JIHAD: WHY, HOW, AND WHEN

ALSO BY QAZI FAZL ULLAH

Sharia & Politics

Ramadan: Components of the Holy Month

Science of Hadith

Hajj and Umrah According to All Four Schools of Jurisprudence

Sayyidah Aaisha: Age & Marriage

Jesus in the Quran

JIHAD: WHY, HOW, AND WHEN

WRITTEN BY **QAZI FAZL ULLAH**

EDITED BY **SHAYLA EDWARDS**

AND **EVELYN THOMPSON**

HUND INTERNATIONAL PUBLISHING

LOS ANGELES, CALIFORNIA

2018

COPYRIGHT © 2018 BY QAZI FAZL ULLAH

All rights reserved. This book or any portion thereof may not be reproduced or used in any manner whatsoever without the express written permission of the publisher except for the use of brief quotations in a book review or scholarly journal.

FIRST PRINTING: 2018

ISBN 978-1-7326017-7-2

HUND INTERNATIONAL PUBLISHING

LOS ANGELES, CALIFORNIA

PRINTED IN THE UNITED STATES OF AMERICA

"AND DO "JIHAD" IN (THE CAUSE OF) ALLAH THE RIGHT (TRUE) JIHAD OF HIM (22:78)."

TABLE OF CONTENTS

- PROLOGUE 9
- THE WORLD AND ITS SUBJUGATION 14
- HUMANS AND ISLAM 17
- ISLAM IS DEEN 20
- DUTIES AND RESPONSIBILITIES 28
- JIHAD 30
- HUMAN INTELLECT 36
- HUMAN DISTINCTION 38
- HUMAN RIGHTS 41
- JUSTICE 47
- IMPORTANT RIGHTS 49
- RIGHT TO LIVE 50
- RIGHT OF EQUALITY 52
- RIGHT OF FREEDOM 54
- RIGHT OF PRIVACY 57
- RIGHT OF EDUCATION 58
- RIGHT TO WORK, EARN AND OWN 60
- RIGHT TO JUSTICE 62
- RIGHT OF FREEDOM OF THOUGHTS AND EXPRESSION 63
- RIGHT TO PROTECT 65
- RIGHT OF RELIGIOUS CONVICTION 67
- RIGHT OF ASSOCIATION 68
- JIHAD AS AN ISLAMIC CONCEPT 70
- JIHAD IN THE MEANING OF QITAL (FIGHTING) 75

- JIHAD IN ISLAM 80
- VERSES ABOUT JIHAD 81
- CAUSE OF JIHAD 89
- HARABAH 102
- PRE-EMPTIVE WAR 105
- DEFENSE 106
- DARUL ISLAM 111
- SPOILS OF WAR 113
- CEASEFIRE 115
- MUSTAMIN 119
- HUDNAH (TRUCE) 121
- ZIMMAH AND JIZYAH 123
- CONDITIONS FOR ZIMMAH 125
- JIZYAH BUT FOR WHO? 127
- TYPES OF JIZYAH 129
- RATIO OF JIZYAH 130
- RIGHTS AND DUTIES OF ZIMMIS 134
- AHADITH ABOUT ZIMMIS 137
- PRISONERS OF WAR 140
- IS IT A MUST TO HAVE CAPTIVES IN WAR? 143
- WHAT SHOULD BE DONE TO THE PRISONERS? 144
- SLAVERY AND SLAVES 152
- EMANCIPATION OF SLAVES 157
- AL WALA WAL BARA 160
- BOOKS BY QAZI FAZL ULLAH 179
- ABOUT THE AUTHOR 191

PROLOGUE

Humans are basically animals, but gregarious. As animal's humans have desires and anger just as animals do. All animals have desires, wishes, and anger defenses, both domestic and wild, from the sea world or on earth, birds or insects, small or big. Animals use only their bodies, but humans also have intelligence and fulfill their desires or defend themselves using their intellect too. Humans invent some good and useful things as well as some very destructive things. At times they fulfill their desires using very brutal means and to defend themselves they sometimes do so in peaceful ways, but this often depends on who uses what and how. This method is as ancient as humans. One might kill another to fulfill his or her desire, or to defend himself in a fight and battle as ancient as humans themselves.

Now to rule and to regulate humans there may be a system and authority to maintain law, order, and peace, to provide justice, and to provide for humans' needs and necessities. In other words, state and government is a requirement. Thus, throughout history humans have created states, governments, and legal systems. Sometime these are based upon divine rules and principles, while other times they are based upon human approach and intellect.

Human approach is limited or affected by the circumstances, so most of the time it will not meet one's needs. It can be even counterproductive. A system for the good of humans and world in general may be given by such an entity whose knowledge is comprehensive, whose mercy is inclusive, whose power is irresistible and unbiased. These qualities belong to *Allah* alone. Thus, if a state or government is based on divine principles, then the actual ruler is *Allah* and the one in authority is His agent who is bound to obey his orders and his commands and to treat others as a family of *Allah*.

The *Prophet Muhammad* said,

"The creature as a whole is like family to Allah, so the nearest one to Allah is the one who is more kind towards His family."

And as *Allah* is the Creator, the Lord, All-Knowing and All-Wise, so whatever He commands it is good for His creature, even if at times it does not appear beneficial. But the result will be not only good, but the best.

In verse 2:216, *Allah* says,

"Fighting has been adjoined upon you while that is disliked by you, but it may be that you may dislike a thing while that is better for you and it may be that you may like a thing while that will be bad for you, as Allah knows and you do not know (the future and the result)."

For a long time, there has been propaganda spreading that Islam is spread by sword and *Islam* inspires bloodshed and killing. This is especially true now-a-days when the human population has grown a lot and continues to grow, and life has become very artificial in which everyone is looking for luxury, pining for control over natural resources, and fortunately or unfortunately, most of these resources are situated in the *Muslim* world. Unfortunately, *Muslims* neither have the technology, nor the skills, nor the tools to explore the same. So, they need others but these others want to grab these resources altogether or at least to control them. Thus, they attempt to find or create ways to take control. This is successful due to the ignorance and emotionalism of *Muslims* that they are advancing their agenda. So, whenever it is needed, they initiate a campaign of propaganda that *Muslims* are terrorists and *Islam* is terrorism so that whole world stands against *Islam* and *Muslims*. Thus, the *Muslim* countries have been attacked one after the other even though the word of *Islam* itself is derived from *Silm* or *Sal'm* which means peace and security.

For this purpose or to meet their agenda they have also propagated that the term of *Jihad* is used to mean

> *"Those who terrorize the whole world and to kill those who are not Muslims."*

By doing so they put *Muslims* on the defense and propagate fear. These types of tactics are terrorizing tactics. Occasionally, some people do something horrible because of fear. Framing a religion or people of a specific Faith as terrorists has not produced anything good; has only caused the situation to worsen.

The world was not as unsafe before as it is now, especially for *Muslims* living in the West. This has become a double-edged sword: People who live in fear either say what these propagators want them to say, or are apologetic instead of being proud of their Faith and belief. This is counterproductive and it is not good for the world at large. People must be having the facts about the *Muslim* Faith, so that there is no ambiguity about it.

In this book we are trying to make it clear what *Islam* is in its real sense and what is *Jihad*, what it means, why, when and how and for what purpose it is used. Because someone must make it clear.

Allah has made this world very beautiful.

WE CAN MAKE IT A PARADISE OR HELL, SO WHY NOT A PARADISE?

In verse 30:41 of the *Holy Qur'an, Allah* says,

> *"Disorder has overtaken the land and sea because of what the hands of people have done, so He (Allah) may cause them to taste some of what they have done, maybe they will take a U-turn."*

It is our collective responsibility as agents of *Allah* to keep this world safe and secure.

BUT HOW?

This is the billion-dollar question and it needs an answer.

May *Allah* accept this effort and may *Allah* give this world some good. *Amin*!

QAZI FAZL ULLAH

LOS ANGELES, CALIFORNIA

UNITED STATES OF AMERICA

THE WORLD AND ITS SUBJUGATION

This beautiful world that we see did not come into existence automatically or on its own! Even the scientists who deal with matter and material things, recognize that it came into existence from energy that was transformed into matter or came from *"matter"* or from molecules or atom. which they call *"mother atom."* But the question remains unanswered as to how this energy, matter, atom or these molecules came into existence? Scientists should not be blamed for what they say since they do not go beyond *"matter"*, its different forms, its analysis and transformation, and the like. *Allah* is neither *"matter"*, nor *"material"*, so the religious ones among the scientists say that they don't take God with them to their laboratories. This means that God and His entity is not discussed in the laboratory of material science since He is beyond that and He is not the subject of science.

As we said, this world came into existence and an entity known by the name of God or *Allah* has created it. That entity is eternal, All-Mighty, All-Wise.

In verse 7:54 of *Holy Qur'an*, He said,

> "Indeed, your Lord is Allah, the one Who created the heavens and earth in six days and then he rose over the throne. He covers the night with day, chasing it very rapidly, and the Sun and Moon and stars subjugated to His command. Behold, His is the creation and the command (authority). Blessed is Allah, the Lord of Worlds."

Verse 10:3 says,

> "Indeed, your Lord is one Who created the heavens and earth in six days, then He rose over the throne, He runs the system."

Verse 54:49 says,

> "Verily, We have created everything to a (specific) measure."

Verse 41:9-11 says,

> "Say! Do you, indeed, disbelieve in the One Who created the earth in two days and attribute to Him equals, He is the Lord of Worlds. And He placed in it firm mountains over its surface and blessed it and measured therein its sustenance in four days, equally for those who need. Then, He turned to the sky and He said to it and to the earth, come (function) willingly or unwillingly. They both said we come willingly."

In the *Holy Qur'an* there are tens of verses stating that *Allah* has created the whole world and the things therein, and He subjugated all those to humans to use it, and thus He honored them.

Verses 14:32-34 say,

"Allah is the One Who created the heavens and earth and sent down from sky the water and produced thereby fruits as provision for you and subjected for you ships to sail through oceans by His command and subjected for you rivers, and He subjected for you the Sun and Moon pursuing their course diligently and subjected to you the night and day, and He has given (provided) you with all that you ask for (need it) and if you count the favors of Allah you cannot count, and verily, humans are unjust, ungrateful."

Verse 17:70 says,

"And indeed, we created the children of Adam and We have made them rulers on land and sea and We have provided them pure things and we have given them a perfect priority over a lot of what We created.

HUMANS AND *ISLAM*

Now, this status and position is not for free as we know the one who attains a certain position also has responsibilities. So, humans are bound to obey the Commandments of *Allah* like all other creatures obey His *Takweeni* orders and functions accordingly. Since animals do not have intelligence, they perform their natural duties. Humans, however, must obey the legal orders too. Since they are being rewarded or punished accordingly, they are given a free will to do good or bad.

Verse 76:3 says,

> "*Indeed, We have shown him the path to be grateful or ungrateful.*"

In verses 91:7-9 *Allah* says,

> "*And by the self and by the One Who proportioned it, so He inspired it with its wickedness and its righteousness. Indeed, the one who purified it He succeeded, and indeed, he failed who corrupted it.*"

Humans are looking for tranquility. And since tranquility is a quality of the soul, one cannot get it through matter or material things, but only be being in touch with *Allah* as He said in verse 13:28,

> *"Those whose hearts (souls) get satisfaction with the remembrance of Allah. Behold, only with the remembrance of Allah hearts can get satisfaction."*

To be close to *Allah* is the only way to follow His commandments and the teachings of His *Prophet*. The more one follows, closer he gets to Him.

In verse 5:35 *Allah* says,

> *"O you who believe! Be dutiful to Allah and seek "Waseelah" (the means to become closer) to Him and strive hard in His path in order to achieve success."*

There are different types of worship for different purposes, but there are also deeds and actions in our daily life for which we have commandments and rules in the *Deen* of *Allah*. When we practice in accordance with the rules it is considered worship.

And, as we know, *Islam* is the *Deen* and only *Deen*. There is no other substitute word for *Deen* in any other language, since this is not a word but a term and title given to *Islam*. The word *"religion"* refers to a belief in some being, but it is also used for superstitions and myths and for a set of rituals. Therefore, it cannot qualify the meaning of *Deen* because that is a perfect and complete system, and in verse 3:19 *Allah* says,

> *"Indeed, to Allah "Deen" is (only) Islam."*

Thus, *Deen* is only *Islam* and only *Islam* is the *Deen*. This *Deen* belongs to *Allah*.

In verse 39:3, *Allah* says,

> "Behold, to Allah belongs the pure "'Deen'" (this is the pure "Deen)."

This *Deen* began with *Adam* and moved towards completion and perfection through all messengers and was completed with the Message of *Prophet Muhammad*.

In verse 42:13 *Allah* says,

> "He (Allah) ordained for you as 'Deen' what He enjoined upon Noah and that which We have revealed to you and what We enjoined upon Abraham, Moses and Jesus to keep the 'Deen' straight and not to divide therein."

And in verse 5:3 He says,

> "This Day We have perfected your 'Deen' for you and completed upon you My favor and chosen for you Islam as Deen."

Yes! *Sharia* and rules were different in different times due to circumstances and situations, as in verse 5:48 He says,

> "For each of you We have prescribed a law and a method."

ISLAM IS *DEEN*

As we said before,

Islam is the *Deen* of *Allah* which was the *Deen* of all messengers and that is the *Deen* of humans and for humans in general.

This *Deen* has four major branches as follows:

i. **FAITHS AND BELIEFS:**

a)   BELIEF IN *ALLAH*,

b)   BELIEF IN HIS ANGELS,

c)   BELIEF IN HIS BOOKS,

d)   BELIEF IN HIS MESSENGERS,

e)   BELIEF IN THE LAST DAY OF THIS WORLD,

f)   BELIEF IN *TAQDEER* (PRE-ORDAINED DIVINE LAW),

g)   BELIEF IN LIFE-AFTER-DEATH.

ii. **CHARACTER:**

This has four branches:

a) *ADL* OR SOCIAL JUSTICE, so that no one may do injustice to anyone, or harm or deprive the other of his or her due rights.

b) *IHSAN* OR KINDNESS which means to do good to the creatures of *Allah* and to show kindness to them.

In verse 16:90 *Allah* says,

"*Verily, Allah enjoins you to do Adl and Ihsan.*"

c) *AFW* OR FORGIVENESS to someone who wronged the other, either accidently, by mistake, or even on purpose, but he sincerely feels sorry for it.

Verse 2:199 says,

"*Hold to forgiveness. Command what is right and turn away from ignorance.*"

Verse 2:237 says,

"*And to forgive, that is very close to piety.*"

Verse 24:22 says,

"*And let them forgive and overlook. Do you not wish that Allah should forgive you?*"

Verse 65:14 says,

"*And if you forgive and overlook and cover up (the faults) then verily, Allah is Oft-Forgiving, All-Merciful.*"

Verse 5:13 says,

> "So forgive them and overlook. Verily, Allah likes the doers of good."

d) *SAF'H* OR TURNING AWAY ONE'S FACE FROM SOMEONE, OR NOT TO TAKE NOTICE OF HIS DOING, OR TO OVERLOOK.

This is mentioned in a few of these previous verses because if someone is hard of hearing or stubborn and he neither listens to the other nor admits when he is wrong, then talking to him is not only a waste of time but can also create a fight for no reason. This is why *Allah* says that true slaves of the Most Beneficent (*Allah*) are those when the ignorant (stubborn) address them they say should say *Salam* (verse 25:63) which means they don't want to get involved with them.

Also, in verse 25:72 *Allah* says,

> "And when they pass by the "Laghw" (senseless) they leave it with dignity."

Regarding *AFW* and *SAF'H* there is also room for equal retaliation and revenge, but that does not take someone out of the fold of noble character as *Allah* says about those who believe and place their trust in *Allah*.

Verses 42:37-43 say,

> "Those who avoid enormities and indecencies, when they are angry they forgive. Those who respond to their Lord, perform the prayers they conduct their affairs with mutual consultation they spend from what We have given them for sustenance. And those who are oppressed when

they are wronged they defend (take revenge). And the recompense for an injury is the equal of that, so who forgive and make peace then their reward is with Allah. Verily, He does not like oppressors. And surely, those who defend (take revenge to an equal degree) after he was wronged, then against them there is no cause of blame. The blame is only against those who oppress men with wrongdoing and insolently transgress beyond bounds through the land, for them there is a painful torment. But indeed, who showed patience and forgave, that is an affair of great resolution (strong will)."

These verses make it clear that whether forgiveness is good depends on situation and where an equal retaliation to defend is allowed.

iii. **DEEDS AND ACTIONS**

Humans have two connections and relations, one towards the Creator and the second towards the creature and, especially, their fellow human beings as they are social by nature living with one another.

Therefore, their actions are of two types:

a) IN CONNECTION AND RELATION TO *ALLAH*. These are called *Ibadat* (worship) as this is the only way to get in touch with *Allah* when one believes in Him and accepts His Message along with this pledge of allegiance. These are five in number.

The other four are:

i. PRAYERS – five times a day;

ii. Fasting in the month of *RAMADAN*;

iii. *ZAKAT* or charity incumbent upon the one who has a specific type of saving of a specific amount and gives a specific portion of it to those who are mentioned in *Qur'an* and *Sunnah*.

iv. *HAJJ* – to visit the *Holy Ka'ba* at least once in a lifetime and to perform specific rituals in its prescribed time, if one can afford it.

b) IN CONNECTION WITH FELLOW HUMANS. As we know, people need each other in different ways to fulfill their needs and necessities and to keep the life running smoothly since they are social in nature. These are classified in four branches.

i. FAMILY LIFE AND RULES – As social beings, humans do not only fulfill their desires, they also establish families. Each new family is established based on marriage, so the first thing is marriage.

a) MARRIAGE – Two persons, a male and a female marry each other. They may both make their own choice but must keep in view their values, norms, and relations to their respective families, which means to do involve their families to make the marriage durable since marriage is a lifetime contract in *Islam*.

b) DISPOSAL OF FAMILY AFFAIRS:

Islam did not put any financial responsibility on women as *Allah* said in Verse 4:34 of the *Holy Qur'an* says,

> *"Men are 'Qawwam' of women as Allah has given to some of them virtues over others and as they spend their wealth, so the righteous women are obedient and they*

> *guard in the absence (of their husbands) as Allah has guarded (them or made them guard)."*

Qawwam is derived from *Qayyim* or *Qaa'im* which means the one responsible for a thing, so one's duty is to provide with maintenance and protection as well, and as we know that one who does this may have an authority in the household matters and affairs of the home, and for sure that is the man as he has these responsibilities.

- c) COMPANIONSHIP: They both may live like two companions even when the male person has authority over female. This is not like the authority of a ruler, but that of a companion.

- d) CHILDCARE: As we know that *Allah* has given different qualities to different genders

   as He said in verse 4:32,

   > *"And do not wish for that by which Allah has made some of you to exceed others. For men there is share of what they have availed (naturally), and for women there is a share of what they have availed (naturally) and ask Allah for His bounty (to fulfill your obligations). Indeed, Allah is All-Knower of All-Things."*

- i. This verse means that each gender must be content with what *Allah* has given him or her and must perform the duties prescribed. This is a requirement for a smooth life. Women are endowed with the nature to take care of small children. The father will earn their livelihood and the mother will take care of their nursing and nurturing as she is the first teacher and trainer of her children.

ii. Financial and Economical: They need each other and things in the hands of others they need transactions like sale, purchase, rent, hire, lease, partnership, etc. In this regard *Islam* has given rules and laws, so all these activities must be based on honesty, truthfulness, and professionalism.

The *Holy Prophet* said,

"A truthful, honest businessman shall be with the prophets and people of Truth."

iii. State and Government: As humans are animals by nature, with desires and anger, when they use their intelligence for this desire and anger, they may cause bloodshed and mischief, while *Allah* wants them to live in peace and harmony with each other. Thus, they need a controlling authority to protect them from one another. This authority is called state and government. The state is established on four pillars i.e., a. territory, b. population, c. government and d. sovereignty, while the government consists of three branches:

a) Legislature, which makes laws;

b) Executive, which looks after the laws, and

c) Judiciary, which enforces laws.

This state and government must provide the necessities to everyone regardless of their cast, color, and religion, treat them equally, and provide them peace and justice. This means it may be a welfare states.

iv. International Relations: As every state is an entity and cannot stay and stand still in isolation and loneliness, but must have relations with other states (i.e., *Muslim* states as well as non-*Muslim* states) like individuals having relations with other individuals, *Muslims* and non-*Muslims*.

This relationship must be based on equality, equity, truthfulness, and honesty, as *Allah* and His *Prophet* both ordered this in general so there may not be any deception or cheating or fraud in any way.

DUTIES AND RESPONSIBILITIES

In *Islam Muslims* have two basic duties and these are:

i. *Dawah* and

ii. *Jihad*

<u>DA'WAH</u> means to call and invite people towards *Islam*, because there is no Messenger after *Prophet Muhammad*, and people need to be corrected and reformed, so *Muslims* are bound to correct them.

In verse 3:110 *Allah* says,

> *"You are the best group brought forth for people, enjoining good, preventing vice and believing in Allah."*

Also, in verse 3:104 *Allah* says,

> *"And let there be a group from amongst you who invite towards, enjoining right and preventing vice."*

This call sometimes may be through words, but since actions speak louder than words, *Muslims* may treat non-*Muslims* in a way that others may be convinced to accept the religion because to convert one by force is not allowed.

In verse 2:256 *Allah* says,

"There is no coercion for conversion."

Rather, one should convey the Message to convince a person and attract him convert to *Islam*.

A young Jew used to work for the *Prophet* of *Allah* as a servant who fell sick and was in his last moments. *Prophet* visited him and ask if he would accept *Islam*. He looked at his parents to see their reaction. They told him to obey *Abul Qasim* (the title of the *Prophet*), and he accepted *Islam*, which means the *Prophet* never forced him to take *Shahadah* even if someone was serving him for some period.

The second successor of the *Prophet*, *Umar* had one Christian servant named *Asbaq*. Once *Umar* told him that if he would accept *Islam*, we could use his good offices in Christian community. He said and referred to the above verse that there is no coercion in conversion. *Umar* said,

"Yes, you are right."

JIHAD

This word is derived from *Jah'd* or *Juh'd* which means effort or striving hard for a legitimate cause, reason, and purpose, especially when that is incumbent upon someone. But sometimes the cause, reason, and purpose requires a fight. When this is so people explain and interpret it in a different way and thus it can have both positive and negative connotations. Yes, sometimes it is misused or even abused, but it is also often avoided even though it has become unavoidable and inevitable, either because of fear or because of vested interests and such people would then say that

> "There is no Jihad, but behind an 'Imam' (legitimate leader)."

Yes, it is right that without a legitimate leader that will cause a mischief, but this is also a maxim that there is no *Imam* but with *Jihad*, which means that *Imam* must have the ability and capability of *Jihad* to protect and defend the state, the public, and the ideology. If he cannot or does not do so, then he will lose his credibility. But even with the eligibility to be an *Imam*, sooner or later he will give up and he will lose the state and its sovereignty; in the same way the people will lose their property, honor, dignity, and even their lives, which is one's duty and responsibility to protect and defend. Moreover, when people feel that the state and *Imam* are not going to defend them, they take it in their own hands, thus many groups begin fighting, which will rarely produce any durable positive results because a fight amongst themselves will only result in turmoil, which not only causes trouble to the specific area, but to the entire world and the world becomes an unsafe place.

Dr. Martin Luther King Jr. said,

> *"We are tied to each other in one single garment, so something which affects one directly affects others indirectly."*

The whole world has become one global village due to the current technologies and inter-state economic and political relations. To misuse or abuse this religious concept is only wrong, and to deny, refuse or condemn it is even worse.

Because of the situation, sometimes the word may lose its definitions, but still the words and terms will still be used with an ambiguity and confusion to them.

Thus, someone must come forward and explain the actual concepts. By doing so, he can bring some good to the people involved in the situation and perhaps they will understand or try to understand the reality. This why we explained *Islam* as *Deen* to help people understand that the concept of *Jihad* is not an invented concept but a divine and revealed concept and one of the basic duties of *Muslims*.

Imam Tirmizi narrated a *Hadith* that *Muaaz Ibin Jabel* said to *Prophet* –

> "O Messenger of Allah tell me of an act which will take me to Paradise and it will keep me away from the Hellfire."

He said:

> "You have asked me about a major matter, yet it is easy for him for whom Allah Almighty makes it easy. You should worship Allah associating nothing with Him; you should perform prayers; you should pay Zakat; you should fast in Ramadan; and you should make pilgrimage to the House.

Then he said:

> "Shall I not show you the gates of goodness? Fasting is (like) a shield; charity destroys sin like water extinguishes fire; and the praying of a man in the darkness of night.

Then he recited:

> "Who forsake their beds to cry unto their Lord in fear and hope, and spend of that what Allah has bestowed on them. No soul knows what is kept hidden for them of the joy as a reward for what they used to do."

Then he said:

> "Shall I not tell you of the peak of matter, its pillar and its topmost part? I said, yes, O Messenger of Allah."

He said:

> *"The peak of the matter is Islam; the pillar is prayer; and its topmost part is Jihad."*

Then he said:

> *"Shall I not tell you of the controlling of all that?" I said, yes, O Messenger of Allah, and he took hold of his tongue and said: "Restrain this. I said, O Prophet of Allah, will that what we say be held against us?"*

He said:

> *"May your mother be bereaved of you, Mu'adh! Is there anything that topples people on their faces - or he said on their noses – into Hellfire other than the harvests of their tongues?"*

This *Hadith* along with others make it clear that *Jihad* is an ongoing concept of *Islam* and the *Zirwatus Sanam* i.e., high hump of *Islam*, and this hump is considered the beauty of a camel and bull and based on its height – higher the hump, higher its price!

And as we have said, *Islam* is the *Deen*. *Deen* means a perfect and complete system, so one may not pick-and-choose. But it is a package.

Verse 2:208 of the *Holy Qur'an* says,

> *"O you who believe, enter in Islam completely and follow not in the footsteps of 'Satan.' Indeed, he is your clear enemy."*

Through these details, it has become clear that when a state is established based on a specific ideology, and that ideology has its own details for each field, then all these fields are linked to each other and a state is bound to defend itself. When an *Islamic* state defends itself, that is called *Jihad* — which is the name and title given to this struggle by Islam itself. And each living entity defends itself and each human individual or group of individuals defends itself. They may be Jews, Christians, Buddhists, Hindus, *Muslims*, or even atheists as this trait is based on their animalistic instincts. They have intelligence and intellect, so their fight or defenses may not be lawless. There must be known rules and laws, limits and bounds. Otherwise, there will be cruelty and brutality—which must be stopped.

Let us now examine what is *Jihad* in *Islam*; when it will take place, and how it will be done.

As we mentioned before, any good effort for a good cause is called *Jihad*. It is used in the same sense in *Sharia* i.e. *Qur'an* and *Sunnah*, which are the two basic sources of law in *Islam*. As far as fight and battle are concerned, sometimes *Sharia* uses this word as well. Otherwise, *Qur'an* and *Sunnah* use the word *Qital*, while sometime *Qital* could be *Jihad* and some other times it will be a *Qital* and fight because, for *Jihad*, one would be rewarded as that is a way of *Ibadah* and worship of *Allah*. *Ibadah* in its broader sense means to do whatever you do in accordance with *Sharia*, the *Qur'an*, and *Sunnah*. If a fight is not in a legitimate way in the light of *Qur'an* and *Sunnah*, or it is not for the good cause of *Allah*, then the person or persons would be punished for it by *Allah*, not rewarded. Yet, if someone does it by mistake due to some deduction or analogy, he has an excuse.

Defense is a natural phenomenon. It cannot be changed. If one tries to change it or tamper with it, the effects could be disastrous. The sole Creator of this universe, *Allah*, has sent divine rules and laws to channelize nature, to polish it and to make it beneficial or less harmful as everything in this world has a good side and a bad side.

Islam orders what is more good than bad and when the bad side is more prevalent, *Islam* prohibits that as in verse 2:219 of the *Holy Qur'an Allah* says,

> *"They ask you about wine and gambling, say in these both there is a big sin and some benefits for people. But its sin is bigger than its benefits."*

HUMAN INTELLECT

Allah has created human in different shapes and with different features and he has given them a different nature. His nature is a combination of animals and angels.

The *Prophet* of *Allah* said,

> "*Verily, Allah has created animals and put therein them natural the desire, he created angels and put therein them nature, the intellect and he created humans and put therein the desire and intellect both. So, the one whose intellect prevails his desire, he is high than the angels and whose desire overtakes his intellect he is lower than animals.*"

Both elements are present and pull and push against each other. There is a continuous fight in the human body. Every time one's desire tries to pull him towards animalistic nature, his intellect pulls him towards angelic nature. Thus, he can become like an animal, even wild, as he is living in a world of desires. *Allah* doesn't want him to be an animal, nor does He want him to be an angel; rather He wants him to be a human in the proper sense in which case his position will be higher than angels. This is possible only if he controls his desires.

Islam does not kill his desires as human, but it tests and tries him with two opposing powers fighting each other and the good one prevail to take over. That is why we say that *Allah* sent *Prophets* and messengers to make humans by feature as human by nature and character.

The *Prophet* said,

"*Indeed, I have been sent to perfect the noble character.*"

This character is meant in prosperity and adversity, as well as in war and peace.

HUMAN DISTINCTION

Allah has given humans intellect, so humans have three distinctions from animals:

i. All Animals look for how to fulfill the desires. But humans struggle to fulfill their intellectual demands as well.

ii. Animals fulfill their desires with things suitable to their nature and natural needs. But in its raw shape full of dust and dirt, humans look for cleanliness and beauty for their needs. They want their food to be delicious, their shelter to be clean and beautiful, and for their mates to be pretty and handsome.

iii. Because humans have intellect, they try to get a lot for little efforts, so those who are smart, creative, and wise invent things; and those who cannot, they adopt the inventions of others for their use. Since the level and approach of their intellect is different, they will have different opinions, which can sometimes lead to fights and battles, as *Allah* has given them a free will that they play with and apply.

In verses 11:118-119 of the *Holy Qur'an Allah* says,

> *"And if your Lord would have willed He would have made mankind one community, but they will keep on differing with each other. But if your Lord has His mercy on someone, and for that He has created them."*

Also, in verse 2:253 of the *Holy Qur'an Allah* says,

> *"And if Allah would have willed, then those who came after them they would not have fought with each other after the clear rules had come to them. But they disputed, so some of them believed and others disbelieved, and if Allah would have willed they would not have fought, but Allah does what He intends."*

Because of this contrast combination in his nature, when *Allah* told His angels,

> *"I am going to appoint on earth an agent."*

They said,

> *"Are you going to appoint the one who will spread mischief there in and he will shed blood while we are there to glorify You along with Your praise and sanctify You."*

He said,

> *"I know what you know not."*

So, *Allah* blessed humans with intellect, so that they would use the world and things therein, but they have been made *Mukallaf* (bound) to obey *Allah* and His commandments.

When they will need things there in the worlds, then for sure differences, disputes and battles will occur, even when *Allah* has commanded them to not spread disorder and mischief.

In verse 7:56 of the *Holy Qur'an Allah* says,

> *"And do not spread disorder on earth after it is set in order."*

In verse 55:7-9 *Allah* says,

> *"And the heavens He raised (built it on a measured light) and set up the balance in order that you may not transgress the balance, and keep up the balance and do not make the balance deficient."*

HUMAN RIGHTS

As brutality, wrongs to people, violation of rights, and deprivation are as ancient as humans themselves, there is always a voice for human rights. Like all other fields, this field is also abused in many ways and certain organizations have been using this voice for their own agenda and vested interests. Thus, those who are sincere in this regard have been exploited, misused, and deceived, especially financially. *Allah*, the sole Creator of the universe in His Basic Message provided liberty and freedom to humans.

The basic Message is

"*La Ilaha Illallah*" (in *Arabic*).

It means

"*There is no god (Lord) but Allah only.*"

This was the Message of all messengers as *Allah* says,

Holy Quran 21:25,

> "And We have not sent any Messenger but We revealed to him that there is no god (Lord but only Me, so worship Me alone (be My slaves only)."

And a companion of the *Prophet, Riba'ee Ibni Aamir* said to an Iranian army general when he asked him about his mission,

> "Indeed, Allah has appointed us to take the slaves of Allah out of the slavery of slaves towards the slavery of their only Lord."

And it is known that only when people will become slaves of *Allah* alone then they will have freedom, liberty, equality and they will be safe and free of every fear.

The whole world agreed upon certain rights these are basic rights. The Message of messengers was to avail these rights for the deprived ones.

In verse 28:5 of the *Holy Qur'an Allah* addresses to *Prophet Musa* (as) to say,

> "And We intended to confer favor upon those who were oppressed in the land (of Egypt) to make them leaders and to make them the inheritors (owners)."

This was the case of all messengers and those who were oppressed and deprived accepted the Message and gathered around *Prophet Musa* (Moses). They faced lots of hardship and difficulties as they believed that this man and his Message could avail them their freedom, honor and dignity. In other words, that we who have been treated very roughly, even worse than animals, can avail our human status through this man and his Message.

When *Prophet Musa* (Moses) came, the first thing he addressed to *Firaun* (Pharaoh) was,

> "So, release to me the children of Israel (7:105 of the Holy Qur'an)."

As this group of people was deprived of their freedom and fundamental rights,

Allah says (28:4)

> "Indeed, Firaun (Pharaoh) exalted himself in the land (of Egypt) and made people in classes, weakening (depriving) a group of them (of their fundamental rights."

Regarding *Prophet Muhammad*, in verse 7:157 of the *Holy Qur'an Allah* said,

> "Those who follow the Messenger they find written (mentioned) with them in 'Torah' and 'Injeel' (Gospel) Who enjoins upon them what is right and forbids them what is wrong and make it lawful for them the good (pure) things and prohibits for them the filthy things and relieves them of their burden and the shackles which were on them."

These shackles are meant to be the shackles of slavery of any type. In divine religion there are five things more precious and valuable and the states and government, must protect that:

i.   LIFE –

The *Prophet* said

> *"The children of Adam are the structure of Lord. Cursed is the one who demolish the structure of Lord."*

He mentioned Lord instead of *Allah*, which implies that the Lord will ask about His structure. That's why *Islam* has introduced the concept of *Qisas* (retribution) to save lives.

Verse 2:179 of the *Holy Qur'an* says,

"And for you in 'Qisas' there is life, O those who have the care of intellect, so you may avoid (killings and murders)."

If a few killers are subjected to retribution, that is sufficient security for society and community.

ii. PROPERTY –

Property is owned in *Islam*; thus, ownership must be given its due respect and be protected. Therefore, *Islam* has fixed severe punishments for theft and robbery, etc.

iii. HONOR –

A prudent person can tolerate so many things such as being harmed physically or financially, but, very rarely he will tolerate if someone harms his honor, respect, and dignity. *Islamic Sharia*, therefore, has fixed punishments for rape, fornication, adultery, and sodomy, etc.

iv. INTELLIGENCE AND INTELLECT IS THE DISTINCTION OF HUMANS.

Thus, they do not tolerate if someone harms him in this regard. Intoxicants are, therefore, prohibited and *Sharia* also punishes their use. Thus, the drug trafficking is a major sin and crime.

v.   FAITH AND BELIEF –

Faith is protected--whether a divine one or created one. When the *Prophet* came to *Medina* and wrote the first ever constitution in human history called *"The Treaty of Medina,"* its articles included:

1. ALL COMMUNITIES SIGNING THE CHARTER WOULD FORM THE COMMON NATIONALITY.

2. IF ANY OF THE SIGNATORIES WERE ATTACKED BY AN ENEMY, OTHERS WOULD COMBINE FORCES TO DEFEND HIM.

3. NO NATIONALITY SHOULD COME INTO TERMS BY ANY SORT OF SECRET TREATY WITH THE *QURAYSH* (PEOPLE OF *MAKKAH*), NOR SHOULD THEY GIVE SHELTER TO ANY OF THEM AND HELP THEM IN ANY OF THEIR DESIGNS AGAINST THE PEOPLE OF *MEDINA*.

4. *MUSLIMS*, JEWS, AND OTHER COMMUNITIES OF THIS REPUBLIC SHOULD BE FREE TO PROFESS THEIR OWN RESPECTIVE RELIGIONS AND PERFORM THEIR OWN RESPECTIVE RELIGIOUS CEREMONIES. NOBODY CAN INTERFERE.

5. INDIVIDUAL AND PERSONAL OFFENSES OF A TRIVIAL NATURE OF ANY NON-*MUSLIM* WOULD BE TREATED AS SUCH AND NO GENERAL LIABILITY WOULD FALL ON THE COMMUNITY TO WHICH THE OFFENDER BELONGED.

6. THE OPPRESSED ONE SHOULD BE PROTECTED.

7. HENCEFORTH BLOODSHED, MURDER, AND INSOLENCE SHOULD BE ABOMINABLE IN *MEDINA*.

8. *MUHAMMAD*, THE *PROPHET* WOULD BE HEAD OF THE REPUBLIC AND, BY VIRTUE OF THIS, HE WOULD BE THE HIGHEST AUTHORITY TO APPEAL IN THE LAND.

Looking at this charter we can say that this was the first written constitution and, also to make it easy to understand, the first *Magna Carta*. It announced the basic and great principles of civic equality, freedom of worship, and religious tolerance. The *Prophet* is the first greatest statesman who realized the importance of the cooperation among people and goodwill in the administration of a country.

In *Islam* the source of law is *Allah* and the law prescribes the rights and duties, thus the source of rights is also *Allah*.

In verse 17:70 of *Holy Qur'an Allah* says,

> "Verily, We have honored the descendants of Adam.
> "This is the decree given by Allah."

Thus, no one can deprive anyone of his due rights as that is against what *Allah* honors. *Allah* has already decreed this for the mankind and those who do not judge by what *Allah* has sent down, they are deniers (verse 5:44); they are the wrongdoers (see verse 5:45); they are wicked (verse 5:47).

JUSTICE

Verse 5:8 says,

> *"O you who believed! Be steadfast witnesses for Allah in Justice and let not hatred of a group tempt you to deal with them unjustly. Deal (with them) justly. That is nearer to piety."*

This concept of equality and justice to all is the Message of *Tauheed*, the oneness of *Allah* that when *Allah* the only one is your Creator and you are the creature. There is no room for discrimination in the world of *Allah*.

Now, when the source of rights is *Allah*, someone has a reserved right on one hand, but on the other hand to avail this right of him may not harm somebody else. This means there are limits and bounds. If someone was playing with his stick swinging it between his fingers and it hits the nose of another, he warns him by saying,

> *"Gentleman, be careful, what are you doing?"*

He may say,

"I am a free man and I play my freedom."

He must know, his freedom ends where the nose of another begins. It is said that freedom is fire—if not contained it will burn you and others.

Now, rights are established in its very origin and could be suspended in circumstances by those who have such authority, but only in such a way which must not harm the human honor and dignity and only in exceptional cases for the good of community and society. In this regard we can say that human rights in a broader sense, were not introduced before *Prophet Muhammad* who is called

"Rahmatul Lil Aalameen,"

meaning a great mercy for the whole worlds (creatures) – see verse 21:107.

IMPORTANT RIGHTS

RIGHT TO LIVE

As we mentioned earlier, no one can take away the life of another for no reason.

Verse 6:151 says,

> *"Slay not the life which Allah has made sacred, but in the cause of Justice."*

Verse 5:32 says,

> *"Whoever killed a human being who has not committed murder or he promoted mischief/disorder on earth, it shall be as if he had killed all mankind, and whoever saved the life of one it shall be as if he has saved the life of all mankind."*

Also, verse 2:179 says,

> *"And for you in "Qisas" (retribution) there is life."*

The first two verses emphasize the importance of giving everyone the right to live, and the third verse makes it clear that all humans are equal in the eyes of divine law, as well as in the eyes of *Allah*. The *Prophet* of *Allah* in his Farewell address at *Arafat* in *Hajj* said:

> *"O People, lend me an attentive ear, for I know not whether, after this year, I shall ever be amongst you again. Therefore, listen to what I am saying to you very carefully and TAKE THESE WORDS TO THOSE WHO COULD NOT BE PRESENT HERE TODAY. O People, just as you regard this month, this day, this city as Sacred, so regard the life and property of every Muslim as a sacred trust. Return the goods entrusted to you to their rightful owners. Hurt no one so that no one may hurt you. Remember that you will, indeed, meet your Lord, and that He will, indeed, reckon your deeds. Allah has forbidden you to take usury (interest), therefore all Interest obligation shall henceforth must be waived. Beware of Satan, for the safety of your religion. He has lost all hope that he will ever be able to lead you astray in big things, so beware of following him in small things. O People, it is true that you have certain rights with regard to your women, but they also have rights over you. If they abide by your rights then to them belongs the right to be fed and clothed in kindness. Do treat your women well and be kind to them for they are your partners and committed helpers. And it is your right that they do not make friends with anyone of whom you do not approve, as well as never commit adultery."*

RIGHT OF EQUALITY

In his sermon *Prophet* said,

> *"There is no virtue (priority) for an Arab over a non-Arab, nor for a non-Arab over an Arab, nor for a black one over a red one, nor for a red one over a black, all of you are from Adam and Adam was from clay."*

Many verses of the *Holy Qur'an* say

> *"Badu'kum min Badin,"*

which means equal to each other.

Moreover, *Allah* says, *Quran 49:13*

> *"We created you all from one male and one female,"*

Which means *Adam* and *Eve* are the genealogical parents of everyone, so all of you are from *Adam* and *Eve* and only later does everyone have only one father and one mother. The famous story in *Ahadith* is that of *Fatimah Makhzoomiyah* who was charged for theft. The family and the tribe brought *Osamah Ibn Zaid*, who was as much liked to the *Prophet* as *Hassan* and *Hussain*, to intercede and pardon her.

The *Prophet* said,

> *"You do intercede in the rules of Allah. I swear by Allah, if Fatimah, the daughter of Muhammad would have done the same I would have severed her hand, and said people before you were perished because if a common man would have committed theft they severed his hand and if a dignitary would have done it they pardoned him."*

It means their discrimination.

RIGHT OF FREEDOM

As we mentioned before, *Tauheed* means freedom from slavery of fellow humans and submitting to *Allah* alone Who is the real Lord and Master. Slavery was an ongoing practice that could not be dropped single-handedly. The enemies will enslave *Muslim* captives but *Muslims* will not, which means that slavery is not introduced by *Islam*, rather it was reformed in that the *Prophet* said,

> *"Be kind to your slaves and treat them as you treat your own family members."*

This is how the companions of the Messenger did. They educated their slaves and their children in such a way that they became *Imams* or leaders and authorities in the *Deen* of *Islam*. *Abdul Malik*, the *Umayyad Khalifa* asked *Zuhari*, the compiler of *Ahadith* where he visited He answered, a few big cities.

Abdul Malik said, who is an authority at *Makkah*? He replied – (1) *Ata Ibni Abi Rabah*. He asked he is from *Arab* family or from slave family. He said from slave family. He asked who at *Yemen*. He said (2)

Tawus Ibni Keesan. He asked about him. He said, slave family, so he told him in *Misr* (Egypt) that there is (3) *Yazeed Ibni Abi Habib* from slave family in *Sham* (Syria). (4) *Mak'hool* from slave family at *Jazeera* between *Tigris* and *Euphrates* rivers there is (5) *Maimun Ibni Mehran* from slave family in *Khorasan*, (6) *Dahhak Ibni Muzahim* from slave family in *Basrah*, (7) *Hassan Ibni Abil Hasan Al Basri* from slave family. In the end, when he asked him about *Kufa*, he told him about (8) *Ibrahim An Nakha'e* that he is *Arab* and not from slaves.

This means that, on one hand, the noble companions of the Messenger – *Sahabahs* - educated these slave families, and on the other hand these slaves or their children preserved this *Deen* and served it. This indicates that while their title was slave, they were not treated as slaves, but you can say like princes, a slave who works and serves his Master he cannot spare that much time to achieve specialty of knowledge in different sciences of *Deen*. *Islam* inspired and encouraged people to set slaves free and provided them a certain way to gain freedom such as different types of *Kafarat* in *Islam* everyone is innocent until proven guilty and an innocent could not be imprisoned in any way, nor be charged for the wrong of another, even if they are closely related to each other.

In verse 6:164 *Allah* says,

> "No bearer of burdens shall be made to bear the burden of another."

Everyone has the right to defend himself, thus backbiting is considered a major sin because the person concerned cannot defend himself. The son of the governor of *Misr* slapped a common man in *Bazar* as his ride overtook the governor's son's ride. He complained to *Caliph Umar* who summoned them to *Medina* and where the accused could not defend himself but admitted to it, *Umar* asked the common man to slap him in the same way in front of people and then he addressed the governor and his son that

> *"their mothers delivered people free, so since when you thought they are your slaves."*

RIGHT OF PRIVACY

No one has any right to interrupt the privacy of others.

In verse 24:27-28 of the *Holy Qur'an Allah* says,

> *"O you who believe! Enter not houses other than your own houses without first announcing your presence and saying "Salam" (greetings) to the dwellers, that is better for you so that you may be heedful and if you find none therein, still enter not until permission is given and if it is said unto you to leave then you may leave as it is good for you and Allah knows what you do."*

RIGHT OF EDUCATION

Seeking knowledge was the first ever revelation:

"Read in the name of your Lord who created (the whole world). He created humans from clot. Read and your Lord is the Most generous, the one Who taught with pen. He taught humans what they did not know."

Thus, the order is twice given to read. Also, He mentioned the pen and that humans will know what they didn't know. Education, therefore, is the right of humans in general. Education will be a continuous process and creative one as *Adam* has been given priority over angels, because he mentioned the names of things and its use as well. So, human knowledge is creative and spreads. Regarding worldly attachments, *Islam* orders to be content with what one has and not to be greedy.

But *Allah* told his *Prophet* in verse 20:114,

"And say, O my Lord, increase Me in knowledge."

The *Prophet* encouraged people to seek knowledge as he said,

"The one who takes a path seeking knowledge therein Allah will make it easy for him to take a path that leads to Paradise (Bukhari)."

And in verse 39:9 *Allah* says,

"Are those who have knowledge equal to those who do not have knowledge? Indeed, only those who have sense can understand it."

Also, in verse 58:11 *Allah* says,

"Allah will exalt those to high ranks who believed amongst you and those who have knowledge."

RIGHT TO WORK, EARN AND OWN

In verse 55:33 *Allah* says,

> *"O the assembly of Jinns and humans if you can enter there in the diameters of heavens and earth, then enter, but you cannot enter except with power."*

Thus, one must get and gain that power to explore resources and to earn not only for himself, but for others too.

In verse 67:15 *Allah* says,

> *"He is the one who made earth subservient to you, so go into its shoulders."*

The *Prophet* said,

> *"The earning one is the beloved of Allah."*

He also said,

> *"Charity is not lawful for a rich one, nor for a healthy one,"*

Which means one who can work and earn but does not. This is one of the duties of the government—to provide earning opportunities for people.

Now, when one earns he owns it for sure and no one can deprive him of his ownership.

In verse 4:29 of the *Holy Qur'an Allah* says,

> *"Do not eat up the properties of one another amongst yourselves, but if that is by trade with mutual consent."*

RIGHT TO JUSTICE

Allah dislikes injustice, even towards one's enemy.

Allah said,

"Do justice that is closer/nearer to piety." (see verse 5:8)

In verse 57:25, He says,

"We surely sent our messengers with clear rules and we sent down with them the Book and the Scale (balanced system of Justice), so that mankind may stand (establish) with Justice."

RIGHT OF FREEDOM OF THOUGHTS AND EXPRESSION

Mankind is intelligent and *Allah* created nothing without a purpose or reason. Intelligence is to think, reflect, and ponder. When someone thinks, then for sure he will express. These are natural instincts and nature may not be constrained.

In verses 55:1-4 *Allah* says,

> *"The beneficent is the one Who taught Qur'an. He created humans and taught them to express."*

The *Prophet* said,

> *"Whosoever wants to speak he may speak good or keep quiet."*

The *Prophet* said to *Muaaz*,

> *"Shall I not tell you the control of all."*

He replied,

> "Yes."

So, the *Prophet* took hold of his tongue and said,

> "Restrain this."

He asked,

> "Would it be held against us what we say?"

The *Prophet* replied,

> "May your mother be bereaved of you. Is there anything that topples people on their faces?"

or, he said,

> "On their noses into Hellfire other than the harvest of their tongues."

This means that freedom of speech must not be used to insult.

RIGHT TO PROTECT

Since everyone has his own authority in his individual capacity, those who rule them cannot deprive them of their right of oppose rulers who do something wrong. The public has the right to speak to oppose and protect in a reasonable and legitimate way. When *Abu Bakr* became *Khalifa*, in his very first address he said,

> *"Cooperate with me as long as I am on the right path and correct if I make a mistake. Obey me as long as I follow the commandments of Allah and his Prophet, but turn away from me if I deviate."*

And *Umar* once said,

> *"If I order you what Allah or the Prophet or Abu Bakr has decreed. They said, "We will obey then." He said, "And if I deviate?"*

Then one *Bedouin* stood up waving his sword and said,

"Then we will straighten you up with the edge of our sword."

Umar said,

"Praise be to Allah Who made in people of Umar the one who will straighten him up with the edge of his sword."

RIGHT OF RELIGIOUS CONVICTION

Religious sentiments may be given due respect, because humans have emotional affiliations to their faiths, not to allow them to practice their religion or desecrate their religion will harm these sentiments and result in feuds, turmoil, and disturbances.

In verse 6:108 *Allah* says,

> *"And do not abuse those whom they call upon besides Allah lest exceeding the limits they will abuse Allah out of ignorance. Thus, We have made fair seeming to every people their deeds, then to their Lord will be their return, so He will inform them of what they used to do."*

The *Prophet* gave this right to non-*Muslims* in the *Treaty of Medina*.

RIGHT OF ASSOCIATION

As humans are social by nature, they socialize. Otherwise, they become psychotic and even the culprit who is jailed through court procedures cannot be kept in solitary confinement, as this is against his/her natural rights. Also, humans do and want to do things, but some things could not be done on individual basis but by a group of people. Now this group, if organized under certain rules, it will be more useful and productive, which is good for the community, society, state, and public. Thus, they have all the right to assemble, associate, and constitute organizations and parties. In this regard, anything that is constructive and for the good of an individual, and does not harm the society and is legitimate, could be considered a right.

JIHAD AS AN *ISLAMIC* CONCEPT

All these details will make it clear that *Islam* is the best system for humans in general and *Muhammad* was and is a role model in this regard. It is one thing what *Muslims* or a group of them say or do something, and another thing is what *Qur'an* and *Sunnah* says what the *Prophet* and his guided successors did, which is the real shape of *Islam* and is admitted by the non-*Muslims* even if they have some enmity or prejudice against *Islam*. So, before talking about *Jihad* in *Islam* we would like to quote one philosopher:

George Bernard Shaw, an ardent Socialist and great Irish writer, has said in his book titled <u>*The Genuine Islam*</u>,

> *"Muhammad was by far the most remarkable man that ever set foot on this earth. He preached a religion, founded a State, built a nation, laid down a moral code, initiated numerous social and political reforms, established a powerful and dynamic society to practice and represent his teachings and completely revolutionized the worlds of human thought and behavior for all times to*

come. He must be called the Savior of Humanity. I believe that if a man like him were to assume the dictatorship of the modern world, he would succeed in solving its problems in a way that would bring it much needed peace and happiness. During the short period of twenty-three years of his Prophet-hood, he changed the complete Arabian Peninsula from paganism and idolatry to worship of One God, from tribal quarrels and wars to national solidarity and cohesion, from drunkenness and debauchery to sobriety and piety, from lawlessness and anarchy to disciplined living, from utter bankruptcy to highest standards of moral excellence. Human histories have never been such a complete transformation of people; or a place, before or since, and imagine all these unbelievable wonders in just over two decades. Europe is beginning to be enamored of the creed of Muhammad. In the next century, it may go further in recognizing the utility o that creed in solving its problems. If any religion had the chance of ruling over England, nay Europe; within the next hundred years, it could be Islam."

As we said before, *Jihad* means to strive hard for a noble cause. So, *Dawat* to convey the Message towards *Allah* and convince people and then to convert them is also *Jihad*, and the best *Jihad* in normal circumstances. All messengers started with that, which was their original job and duty. *Tabarani* and *Bayhaqi* narrated from *Abu Omamiah* that in *Hajj* someone asked the *Prophet* about the best type of *Jihad* when he threw pebbles on *Jamarah*. The *Prophet* looked at him without answering him and mounted his she-camel. When the *Prophet* threw pebbles on the second *Jamarah*, that man asked him the same question. The *Prophet* did not answer and mounted his she-camel. After the third and last *Jamarah*, the man did not ask.

So, the *Prophet* asked, where is that man?

He said,

> "Here, o the messenger of Allah."

The *Prophet* said,

> "The best Jihad is the word of truth in front of a cruel authority."

Abu Zar Ghifari once asked the *Prophet* about the best *Jihad* and the *Prophet* said,

> *"To strive hard against yourself and your desires" (which means holding one's own self and controlling his desires) (Deelami).*

Once a farmer came and shook hands with the *Prophet* and others, so one man said regarding his hardworking hands,

> "I wish his hands were hardened for Jihad in the path of Allah."

The *Prophet* said,

> *"If his hands were hardened because of earning lawful provision to feed his small children and to serve his old parents, that is also in the path of Allah,"*

Meaning that is also a type of *Jihad*.

Like *Dawat*, *Jihad* was a continuous practice of the *Prophets*, and was of different shapes and in different ways as *Jihad*, but in the meaning of fight, began when the *Prophet* migrated to *Medina* and established a state there. The concept and order of *Jihad* was given there in *Makkah* as this is seen in *Qur'anic Surahs*, which were revealed before *Hijra*. Some scholars said this was regarding other types of *Jihad* and not to fight because *Muslims* were commanded to show patience and stability, commitment and loyalty. Others said to convey *Dawat*, but we say that the basic concept was given there in *Makkah*, while the order to practice and exercise was given when they came to *Medina*, like the concept of *Hajj* was given before, but the order for practice came in the ninth year after *Hijra*.

In verse 25:52, *Allah* said,

> "So obey not disbelievers but strive hard with this (*Qur'an*) the great *Jihad*."

This *Surah* (chapter) descended in *Makkah*, so *Dawat* with *Qur'an* and countering polytheism with *Qur'an* is called great *Jihad* because

1) It was making them speechless, and

2) the *Prophet* and his *Sahabahs* (noble companions) suffered hardships after this *Dawat*, that is *Jihad*.

This concept is further supported by *Makki Surah* 16:110, which says,

> "Then to those who migrated after that and who are persecuted, they strived hard (did Jihad) and showed patience, indeed, your Lord after that is Oft-Forgiving, Most Merciful."

The scholars said that this migration was the migration to *Habesha* (Abyssinia), and this *Jihad* means their striving hard in *Dawah* and facing torture with patience. A famous *Tabi'ee* (one from the second generation) *Ibrahim Ibin Abalah* said, when coming back from *Jihad*:

> *"We came back from a minor Jihad to a major one (Because in the battlefield you kill others, destroy their structures, fight the apparent enemies while back in your own cities you have to build structures and develop to reform people and provide them peace and means to live and to find out your hidden enemy and to keep an eye on them and restrain yourself and control your desires and these jobs are more difficult than Jihad and fighting in the battlefield).*

JIHAD IN THE MEANING OF *QITAL* (FIGHTING)

The word *Qital* is specific to fighting, while the word *Jihad* is used for this meaning in circumstances. Thus, in *Qital* fight is the must. But this is not killing. But therein the killings take place, In *Jihad* fighting is not a must as sometimes the goal is achieved without fighting. For example, if they accepted *Islam* or if they surrendered or asked for a peace treaty. When *Jihad* is *Jihad*, then that is *Ibadah* (worship) and has a big reward, even if fighting and killing took place. But there must be a very specific, sincere intention for the sake of *Allah* and for His cause. Otherwise, it will get converted to mere *Qital* and this fight will be a cause of punishment on the *Day of Judgment*. Wicked people also do *Qital* and fight while *Jihad* is always by good and noble people for a noble cause. Thus, *Qital* converts to *Jihad* when based on sincere intention and a noble cause.

This is because *Allah* created this world and all things therein, and He does not like *Fasad* (disorder, mischief, destruction), nor does He like *Mufsideen* (those who spread disorder and destruction).

Verse 2:205 says,

"And Allah does not like 'Fasad."

Verse 28:7 says,

"Indeed, Allah does not like Mufsideen."

Jurisprudence Scholars say that *Jihad* itself is *Qabeeh* (vile action). But due to its noble purpose, it becomes a good deed.

But *Jihad* has its pre-requisites –

- When it becomes inevitable and unavoidable,

- Then that is *Fard-e-Kifayah* in normal circumstances, which means collective responsibility of *Muslims*, so some of them will do that,

- There must be an *Imam* to declare that, not to cause turmoil.

Prophet said,

"Verily, Imam is shield to fight behind him" which means under his leadership and command, and this is a must for the unity of followers."

Therefore, it is said that there is no *Jihad* but behind an *Imam*. If there is no single *Imam*, the fight mostly disturbs and destroys the system, the infrastructure, and the control, and causes anarchy and a bad system of government is better than anarchy as people become wild in that case. On the other hand, if *Jihad* has become unavoidable and inevitable and the *Imam* does not declare it and does not want to launch it, the maxim is that

"There is no Imam without Jihad"

because people will try to defend their lives, properties, honors, and faith. This will create the same type of turmoil, but even worse. So many leaders will come forward without any eligibility, skill, and scrutiny, and nobody will know who wants what. The situation will be simply exploited and the *Imam* will lose control and authority and be dethroned and others will take over. Then, mostly they will not be able to stand still, as warriors without any proper structure, order, or system, then other people can takeover. This will be an ongoing practice and as there will be no infrastructure, people will face destitution. The lack of any proper system and government will aggravate the situation further. And since the world has become one global village, people compete to accumulate as much wealth as they can, and in this era of technology every formula is available on internet, so the rich, greedy people will be using these warriors for their own interests and will support them. Mostly the jobless, deprived youth will be used in this regard in the name of an ideology and *Deen*. And some states sometimes use these groups, even constitute groups, and after they've done their job, they discard them. So, these trained people then become a threat to the world and their father states kill them in one name or the other, and thus the situation becomes worst every day. This will be titled terrorism. But who caused it? All of us! So, what is the basic cause of this phenomenon?

In 1963, Dr. Martin Luther King was in jail in Birmingham, Alabama. He wrote a letter to a group of white clergymen who attacked him for his method of fighting racial discrimination. In that letter he defended himself by an appeal to an ancient distinction between a negative peace and a positive peace, which is the presence of justice.

Thus, justice means social justice i.e., the common good of man or the common good of common man, as the elites already have it and get it. This social justice could be availed from divine revelations and discovered from reason by sincere, learned, wise, experienced, skilled people as reason or intellect is the distinctive means of humans for getting knowledge, and *Islam* commands for its use. Such an approach is acceptable to those also who do not believe in the divine rules and could be a common ground for world peace. Human rights are meant to let people live according to their nature and that is to pursue the ends that are proper for them. Now, social justice is the habit or disposition whereby the rights of others to be served, which means looking to the good of others. The good of others is possible only in the framework of common good.

Man, by nature is free and intelligent and he has dignity and deserves reverence from others. He is also social, naturally struggling towards perfection within the society. This is not a competition, but a work inside a family. Still he has his individual side as well, so sometime rivalry and competition and overtaking others overtakes him, but to fulfill his social and individual needs are called the common good. Therefore, we need to share our knowledge and our love with others generously. To the best of my observation, we have been overtaken by extreme individualism and individual interests, which is the primary cause of what is going on—which means action and reaction or counter action—while the whole world has become one society now.

Hafiz Ibni Tamiya used to oppose the governments of his time and was in jail again and again. He died in the jail. Once his disciples told him in jail that they planned to topple the government.

He replied,

> *"Only if you can replace it with a better government,"*

otherwise it will bring a turmoil or at least no good.

French leader Charles De Gaulle once visited *Saudi Arabia* to have a deal for oil. The then Prime Minister of Israel showed his concern about the visit of a friend of them to an enemy country of them. De Gaulle said states believe in interest and not in friendship.

Now, almost all states do the same they use some people for their interest making them warriors and later on dump them. There they are neither under any leadership nor any control so they do what they want or think for their good or their survival or even to release their anger.

Amazingly these states as well as the warriors both sometime use and exploit the name of religion and sometime the title and protection of human rights to make their opponent bad in the eyes of people that what we do this is good and what other opponents do that is wrong.

So, if we do not take that into consideration, this situation will continue and leaders from all over the world must be realistic in addressing the issues, administrating justice on an equal and equitable level, helping the poor and backward states and the people providing them with love and knowledge. As states or people do what they do to be the leaders, with such like tactics they cannot get it wholeheartedly while what we said, that will make them leaders in a good way and with respect.

To reach these goals, sometimes they propagate a lot against a specific community and its faith, even to create hatred against them, so when they will attack them there may not be any voice to be heard for what you say could be or really is the act of a group. So, the whole religion should not be blamed for it. In such a situation, some people ignorantly, while some others as a mindset, attack their faith and condemn the religious concept that group has used or has been using like *Jihad*.

JIHAD IN *ISLAM*

Let's look at *Jihad in Islam*. For sure, this includes *Jihad*, which is used in the meaning of fight. As most scholars said that *Surat Ul Hajj*, chapter 22 of the *Holy Qur'an*, *Makki* surah is revealed before *Hijra* to *Medina* and *Jihad* became mandatory in *Medina* when the state was established, but verses 39 and 40 are *Madani*, which descended after *Hijra* (migration).

VERSES ABOUT *JIHAD*

These verses say, Permission (to fight) is given to those on whom the war is imposed because they are oppressed and *Allah* is fully able to help them. Those who have been turned out of their houses without a just cause, except that they said,

> *"Our Lord is Allah and had there not been Allah's repelling some people by others then certainly, there would have been pulled down monasteries, churches, synagogues and "Masajid" (mosques) in which the name of Allah is commemorated a lot and for sure, Allah will help the one who helps Him (His Deen and cause). Verily, Allah is All-Powerful, All-Mighty."*

Analysis of Verses

(1) As in *Makkah* when *Muslims* were being tortured and *Allah* directed them for patience, stability, and no retaliation, to have the *Dawah* going on and to have more and more people convinced and

converted. Otherwise, they will get involved in the fight without means and resources, and *Dawah* will stop while some people said,

> *"And those who believed used to say, why not a surah (chapter) is sent down (about retaliation and fighting), but when a surah of decisive meaning is revealed and fighting is mentioned therein, you saw those in whose hearts there is disease (weakness, cowardice) looking towards you with a look of one in swoon at the time of death, but more fitting for them was it to obey and say a just word and when a matter is decreed then, if they would have said the truth it would have been good for them (see verses 47:20-21)."*

This verse means that when no fight was ordained and you were asking for fight but when the fight is ordered, then some of you were showing weakness, while *Deen* means obedience with sincerity and truthfulness. If the order is patience and no revelation, then do that; and when the order is to fight then be brave and fight as *Allah* knows what should be the order of the day.

In verses 4:77-78 *Allah* complains to the people,

> *"Have you not looked at those who were told to restrain their hands and perform prayers and pay 'Zakat' (charity)? Then, when the fight was made mandatory for them, behold, a group of them used to fear people like the fear of Allah or even more and they said, 'O our Lord, why you made fighting mandatory for us, why you did not grant us a respite to a near (little) time?' Say, 'the enjoyment of this world is little and the Hereafter is better for the one who fears (Allah), and you would not be dealt*

with unjustly in the very least. Wherever you are, death will find you, even if you are in towers (that are) built very strong and high."

When the order and permission to fight came, then the enemies started propaganda in another way that look now they fight, why?

So, *Allah* said,

"That no fight in Makah."

was the order of *Allah* in the same way this permission is also given by the same *Allah* as the cause and reasons are obvious and manifest, these are:

i. The war has been imposed on them,

ii. A lot of wrongs have been done to them,

iii. They have been turned out of their homes and houses without any just cause, but only because they believed in the lordship of *Allah* while to adopt a faith in a normal way is not a crime that people would be tortured or turned out of their houses because of,

iv. This way *Allah* controls people by one another; otherwise, even the worship places cannot remain safe and secure.

In verse 2:251 He says,

"And if Allah would not have checked (controlled) people by each other, the earth would have been in a state of disorder. But Allah is gracious to the creature."

This verse indicates that in some circumstances the fight is a grace of *Allah* to keep up the order and to maintain peace.

2. In verses 190-193 He says,

> *"And fight in the path (cause) of Allah with those who fight you, and transgress not the limits. Verily, Allah does not like the transgressors and kill wherever you find them and turn them out wherefrom they have turned you out and "Fitnah" is worse than killing. But fight them not near "Masjid al-Haram", (the Sacred Mosque) unless they fight you there, so if they fight you there, then kill them. Such is the recompense of disbelievers. But if they cease (stop), then verily, Allah is Oft-Forgiving, Most Merciful. And fight them until there is no "Fitnah" and the "Deen" becomes (that of) Allah. Then, if they cease, then let there be no hostility, except against those who are wrongdoers."*

Here in the first verse, *Allah* again said that the war is imposed on you and if the enemy started it, there is no choice but to retaliate and no prudent person will condemn you for that retaliation. Yes, still as a *Muslim*, fight is not only a fight for you, but this is a part of your *Deen*, and *Deen* is the system, and the system has rules, limits, and conditions for each and everything. So, you must keep in mind that transgression is neither allowed nor liked by *Allah*. When fighting starts, then sweets are not distributed, but the killing will take place. So, if you will not kill them, they will kill you. So, go ahead and kill. Also, turn them out of their homes as they did to you. And if someone makes an objection to this killing, then tell them that they used to persecute us and they enjoyed it, which was worse. *Fitnah* means persecution. It also has other meanings like conspiracy, plotting, etc., and to counter a plot or conspiracy is a must to save and protect one's own self, his people, their lives, their property, honor, faith, etc., as the case may be and no one has the right to make an objection to this defense and protection. It is a matter of common sense. Yes, *Haram* a limited area around the Sacred *Mosque* in *Makkah* is sacred, so it must not be desecrated by fighting therein, but if they fight you there, again there is no way but to retaliate. And when the fighting starts, then cut off the *Fitnah* completely and do not leave the job undone. This will make the world safer.

Winston Churchill said,

> *"Victory does not mean to capture a hilltop, a seaport or an airport, but to cut off the power of enemy to fight you."*

In verse 194 *Allah* answers their propaganda, as propaganda is the tool of war and it is mostly a lie. That's why it is said that the first victim of war is the truth. Why if one has the fear of *Allah* he will not cheat, nor tell a lie, even in the battle as he does not believe that *"in love and war everything is fair."* This is wrong. This opens a gateway to brutality and *Islam* does not allow brutality. Strategy is something else where you say such a thing that has a double meaning, an obvious one and a deeper one, and if the enemy takes obvious one, then he is deceived on his own self, not by you. He has to blame himself. Does anyone expect support from his enemy in the battlefield? Not at all! As far as *Muslims* are concerned, there are rules and pre-requisites to start a fight, during the fight, and to stop fighting and have a ceasefire or peace treaty. But to cheat or tell a lie even in the battle is not allowed. Yes, certain rules for times of peace are dropped in the battle, such as if they started fight near the *Haram*, *Muslims* may retaliate even though to start a fight, there is a desecration of the *Haram*. It has been the same way for a very long time. Fighting during the sacred months of *Rajab, Zul Qadah, Zul Hajjah* and *Muharram* was not allowed. Polytheists also used to follow this rule and this was the rule in *Islam*. But again, if they fight you in those months, then you may fight as well.

In verse 2:194 it says,

> *"Sacred Month is for the Sacred Month and all sacred things are (under the law of) retaliation, so if anyone transgresses the prohibition against you, then you may transgress against him likewise. But fear Allah and know that Allah is with those who fear Him."*

This verse means that rules are sacred, but under certain circumstances they are relaxed as defense is a duty, rather than to be a mere right. Duty must be performed and fulfilled. But still there are limits and conditions that must be considered. So, exceeding what is permissible for you, is not allowed, and that is what the *Muttaqeen* means in the end of the verse that *Allah* is with them who fear Him and do not exceed when they retaliate.

3. Verse 4:75 says,

> *"And what is the problem with you that you do not fight in the path of Allah, while the oppressed people from men, women and children and those who say, our Lord! Take us out of this city the people of which are oppressive, and provide us from your side a protector and provide us from you a helper."*

This verse means that war is incumbent upon you when people are oppressed and they ask for help. This concept is clarified further in verse 8:72-73 which says,

> *"Indeed, those who believed and emigrated and fought with their wealth and lives in the cause of Allah and those who gave shelter and helped, they are friends (helpers) of each other. And those who believed and did not emigrate,*

then you do not have any responsibility of them till they emigrate. And if they ask help from you in (matters of) "Deen", then help is incumbent upon you but not against a people who have a treaty with you. And Allah is the Seer (watcher) of what you do. And those who disbelieved are helpers of each other. If you do not do this, then there will be a "Fitnah" on earth and a big disorder (mischief)."

These two *Ayat* (verses) make a few points clear:

i. *Muslims* are friends and protectors of each other because of their one and the same Faith, so they may help each other when they are the citizens of one and the same *Muslim* state.

ii. *Muslims* living in non-*Muslim* states are not the responsibility of the *Muslim* state. If they ask for any help regarding *Deen*, then based on Faith you may help them. Now what type of help and against whom?

If *Muslims* have their worldly disputes and not a religious dispute, then there is no responsibility on *Muslims* of the *Muslim* state. They should tackle their issues on their own. If they lack resources and ask for financial help for a place to worship or a school or *Islamic* books, then *Muslim* state may help them. And if they are wronged because of their Faith and they never ask an *Islamic* state for help, then the *Islamic* state may not jump in to aggravate the situation for them even more. And if they ask for help, if the *Islamic* state has a relation or common forum with that non-*Muslim* state, then it should use that forum since attacking that country directly will aggravate the problem and many people will suffer. In such cases, war will be the last resort. Now-a-days the world has so many common forums, even the non-*Muslim* states will raise a voice for the oppressed *Muslims*, then indicating towards this whole procedure, *Allah* said, that if you people will not tackle it this way as for details mentioned above, then there will be a big *Fitnah* and disorder. And as we mentioned before since now-a-days the world is not composed of two countries, it will spread to a bigger part of the world, rather the whole world at large.

CAUSE OF *JIHAD*

When we consider these verses deeply we find the cause of *Jihad* as follows:

i. When *Muslims* are turned out of their homes for no reason, except that they say our Lord is *Allah* i.e., they believe in the lordship of *Allah* alone.

ii. When the war is imposed upon them or started against them.

iii. When the enemy wronged them, they may retaliate.

iv. When the enemy is conspiring against them and their country.

v. When in a non-*Muslim* country, but even in a *Muslim* country, the people are oppressed and they cry for help.

vi. When *Muslims* in a non-*Muslim* country ask for help regarding *Deen*, one must help them in matters of *Deen* under normal circumstances financially for some religious cause. If they are tortured or persecuted because of *Deen* and they ask for help, then a proper forum, if there is any, may be used for that to resolve the issue, but not to aggravate the situation. Now, keeping in view all these points the common cause of action or war is not the *Kufr* that they are not Muslims, but oppression and wrongdoing in one way or the other, and to stop oppression, no one will object to it.

So, this is the point of view of *Jumhur* i.e., three *Imams* (jurists), *Abu Hanifa*, *Malik* and *Ahmad* that the basic cause of war is to counter the *Harabah* (attack or a plan of attack or conspiracy) of the attackers, while according to *Imam Shafi* in one saying, the cause is *Kufr*. *Jumhur* based their point of view on these aforesaid verses 190-194 of *Surat Ul Baqarah* where *Allah* said,

> *"Fight those who fight (against) you and when the war starts in accordance to its pre-requisites, then don't stop it until the "Fitnah" (conspiracy, torturing the oppressed, seduction, sedition, etc.) is uprooted, but transgression is not allowed and also if they stop, then you may stop as well."*

In verse 75 of *Surat Ul An Nisa*, the fight is to help out the oppressed people who cry for help and in verses 39-40 of *Surat Ul Hajj* permission to fight is given to counter the oppression which took place because these oppressed people adopted a Faith and the oppressors did not like it.

And when fighting is necessary, then *Allah* inspires *Muslims* in different ways and in verse 9:13 He says,

> *"Why you do not fight a people who broke their oaths and they are determined to expel the Messenger and they had started it the first time. Do you fear them? So, Allah deserves more to be feared of Him, if you are of believers."*

In verse 4:76 it says,

> "Those who believed they fight in the cause of Allah while those who disbelieved they fight in the cause of "Taghut" (Satan/demons), so fight (against) the friends of "Taghut." Indeed, the plot of "Taghut" is weak."

In verse 9:36 it says,

> "And fight (against) the polytheists collectively as they fight (against) you collectively."

In this verse the wording

> "as they fight (against) you collectively"

means they started it. Also, there are *Ahadith* of the *Prophet* in this regard:

1. *Hanzalah Al Katib* says that we fought in the company of *Prophet*, so we passed by a woman who was killed and people gathered around. People made a place for the *Prophet* – gave him an access among them, so he said, she was not fighting among those who were fighting, then he said to one person,

   > "Go to Khalid Ibni Waleed and tell him that the Prophet commands you not to kill Zurriyah or workers (slaves) (Ahmad, Abu Dawud Ibni Majah)."

   Then *Bukhari* and *Muslim* narrate a *Hadith* on the same subject. This is after the battle of *Hunain*. *Ibni Hisham* said that the world *Zurriyah* here means women. Literally, it means children.

2. *Abu Dawud* related from *Anas* that the *Prophet* said,

> "March ahead in the name of Allah but do not kill an old one or a child or a woman. Do not cheat in spoils of war, collect your booties together, do "Islah" and be kind. Verily, Allah loves kind people."

The word *Islah* means right action as needed. It also means to reconcile or to agree to a peace treaty in the field and may be addressed justly and accordingly as

Allah says in verse 8:61,

> "And if they incline to peace then you incline to it as well, and rely upon Allah. Verily, He is All-Hearing, All-Knowing."

But one point must be made clear that in Islam it is very difficult to launch a war as it has so many pre-requisites and condition. But once it starts then to stop it and to cease is also difficult, as wars could not be launched every day, so now it should be taken to its logical result, which is to uproot the *Fitnah* and to retain and maintain peace.

So, in verse 47:35 *Allah* says,

> "So do not be weak, nor ask for peace as you are high, Allah is with you and He will never deprive you of your deeds."

This verse makes it clear that when the war is started, fight wholeheartedly and do not cry for peace. You are high in one way or the other means victory or martyrdom in the cause of *Allah*. Victory is a success here in this world and martyrdom is a success in the Hereafter.

When the hypocrites at the time of the *Battle of Tabuk* said *"wait,"* these *Muslims* will be killed by Roman.

In verse 9:52 *Allah* said,

> *"Tell them, you do not wait for us but one of the two best (martyrdom or victory)."*

Yes, it depends on the situation and circumstances. If *Muslims* think they need a peace treaty then we, as *Muslims*, can do it, but not in a humiliating way.

Thus, *Allah* said,

> *"And Allah is with you"*

to encourage them.

3. *Tabarani* narrated that when *Abu Bakr*, the first successor of the *Prophet* was sending *Osamah Ibni Zaid's* army as the *Prophet* had ordered at the time of his death, he told him,

> *"Do not cheat, nor deceive, nor steal from the booty, nor mutilate the dead bodies, nor kill a child or an old man or a woman, and when you pass by a people devoted to monasteries, then leave them along with what they have devoted themselves for." It means neither these monks be disturbed, nor their practices."*

In brief, these verses and *Ahadith* say that non-combatant people may not be killed in any way, even if they are disbelievers. But *Imam Shafi'* for what he said i.e., that disbelief is the cause of war, so war may be launched against them because of disbelief.

He referred to the following verses:

1. Verse 9:5 says,

> "Then kill the polytheists wherever you find them and capture them and set in wait for them in every place of ambush. But if they repent, pray prayer, give "Zakat" (charity) then let them be free. Indeed, Allah is Oft-Forgiving, Most Merciful."

2. Verse 9:30 says,

> "Fight those who do not believe in Allah and the Last Day and who do not consider unlawful what Allah and His Messenger have made unlawful and who do not adopt the religion of Truth from those who were given the Scripture until they give "Jizyah" willingly while they are humbled."

Jizyah is a specific amount the *Islamic* state is taking from its non-*Muslim* citizens or subjects as *Muslims* are already paying to the state a few types of charities. These charities and taxes are the revenues of the state with which the state is providing its citizens facilities and protection.

Abu Dawud and *Tirmizi* narrated from *Smurah*, son of *Jundub*, that the *Prophet* said,

> "Kill the polytheists' "Shuyukh" and leave their children."

In the books of *Ahadith* and *Seerah* it is mentioned that the *Prophet* declared 15 people of *Makkah* to be killed wherever they are found. This was at the time of the conquest of *Makkah*.

They were *Abdullah Ibni Abi Sarah, Ikramah Ibni Abi Jah'l, Huwairith Ibni Naqeed, Miqyas Ibni Dubabah, Habbar Ibnul Aswad, Kab Ibni Zuhair, Harith Ibni Hisham, Zubair Ibni Umayyah, Safwan Ibni Umayyah, Wahshi Ibni Harb* and four women named *Qareebah, Fartanah, Sara, Hind Binti Otbah.*

So, *Shafi'* said that the *Prophet* declared them to be killed because of their *Kufr* (disbelief). But in the beginning of verse 9:5 *Allah* said,

> *"When the sacred months are passed then kill the polytheists."*

And in verses 9:6-8 it is said,

> *"And if any of the polytheists ask your protection, then grant him protection, so that he may hear the words of Allah – (the book) then take him to his place of safety (his country's boundaries and hand him over to his people). That is because they are a people who do not understand. How can there be any treaty for the polytheists in the eyes of Allah and His Messenger except for those with whom you made a treaty at the Masjid al-Haram, so as long as they are upright towards you, be upright towards them. Indeed, Allah likes the pious. If they gain dominance over you they will not observe in your case any kinship or any covenant of protection. They will try to make you happy with their mouths (words) while their hearts refuse (that) and most of them are wicked (outlaws)."*

So, in these verses,

i. Protection to one who asked for it, is mentioned while still he is a polytheist;

ii. This is also mentioned to take him back to his own people safely while he is *Mushrik*;

iii. Exemption to those *Mushrik* who are living in the *Haram*, to fulfill your treaty with them and they are *Mushrik*;

iv. The context says that they will never honor the treaty when they have a chance. But you may take care of them and verse 9:29 says that they may be given protection when they agree to pay the *Jizyah*. Their lives, properties, honors and even their faith and religious places and practices are protected.

Then there is the *Hadith* of *Abdullah Ibni Umar* that the *Prophet* said,

> *"I have been commanded to fight against people till they testify that there is no god but Allah and that Muhammad is the Messenger of Allah, and they perform the prayer, pay "Zakat", so when they did it, then their bloods and their properties are protected from me, but only when Islam allowed that."*

In the *Hadith* there is a word *Oqatilu* from *Muqatalah*, and that is for fight from both side, so it means they imposed it on me. So, now I will fight till they accept *Islam*, or as we mentioned, accept the *Jizyah*, which means they accepted a rule and system of *Islam* so the non-*Muslim* citizens of a *Muslim* state who submitted to the state and its constitution are called *Zimmi* or protected citizens and constitutional *Muslims*, even though faith-wise they are still disbelievers. And, as we said, there are certain conditions and pre-requisites for *Muslims* to start a war. Moreover, certain scholars have advanced their reservations regarding this *Hadith*–if this is *Sahih* or not. Because the very narrator of this *Hadith*,

Ibni Umar, did not mention this *Hadith* when his own father *Umar* disagreed with *Abu Bakr* when he was going to launch a war against those who refused to pay *Zakat* (charity) to the state right after the death of the *Prophet*.

Umar said,

> "*You are going to launch a war against those who testify that there is no god but Allah and Muhammad is the Messenger of Allah!*"

Abu Bakr said,

> "*I will do that against the one who will differentiate between prayer and "Zakat" i.e., he prays but denies "Zakat."*"

But for the acceptance of this *Hadith*, this is enough that *Bukhari* and *Muslim* both narrated it. So, the basic point is this word *Oqatilu* used in this *Hadith* like as Arabs say,

> "*La oqatilanna ha olai Ala irzi was mumtalakatl.*"

For sure, I will fight these people on my honor and properties. Here, also the word *Oqatil* is used in the word *Oqatilanna*, which means they have attacked my honor and properties and the *Prophet* also said at Hudaibiyah –

> "*La oqatilannahum Ala Amri Haza.*"

I will fight them on this affair of mine, as the *Prophet* said to *Budail Ibni Warqa*, who was trying to make a peace treaty between *Prophet* and the people of *Makkah* as these people were proceeding towards a war. So, now the word *Oqatilu* means I will retaliate and counter what they do. *Imam Shafi'* himself said, *Qital* is not *Qatl* i.e., killing, but countering and fighting. So, there can be *Qital* without *Qatl* like as there can be some *Qatl* without *Qital* as if someone killed another for no reason or for a reason but not in a *Qital* (battle).

In verse 49:9 *Allah* said,

> *"And if two groups of believers fought with each other, make a peace between them, then if any one of them wrongs, then fight the one who wronged until it came back to the order of Allah."*

The verse said, *"Fight"* and it did not say *"Kill."* *Ibni Hajar* relates from *Ibni Daqeequl Eid* that permission to fight is not permission to kill.

Then look! For a *Muslim* who does not pray nor pay *Zakat*, *Islam* does not allow his killing even though he is breaking his pledge as this is mandatory for him to pray and to pay *Zakat*. The non-*Muslims* have not given their pledge yet, then how their killing could be permitted.

The *Hadith* of *Smurah* said, kill the polytheists *Shuyukh*, so *Shuyukh* means skillful planners of war as they are combatants. But the base and foundation of *Shuyukh* is known from the other word in the same *Hadith* and leave their *Sharakh*, which means the children, so *Shuyukh* means their elders and planners.

As far as the case of the declaration of the killing of these fifteen people is concerned, it was not because of their *Kufr* and disbelief. Otherwise, all the people of *Makkah* were disbelievers, but this was due to some other reasons as some of them had committed high treason such as *Ibni Khatal*. He accepted *Islam* then he defected to the people of *Makkah*. He used to write derogatory poetry against *Islam*, against the *Prophet* and *Muslims*, even advancing stories of disrepute against *Muslim* women, which his two singer girls, *Qareebah* and *Fartanah*, used to sing. That's why when he rushed to *Ka'ba* looking for refuge and the companion of the *Prophet* saw him there and came to the *Prophet* saying, I had to cut him but he got away for shelter in *Ka'ba*. He was told to go there and kill him there. His crime was too serious to get shelter in *Ka'ba*, so his killing was not because of *Kufr* and disbelief but he stayed amongst *Muslims* as a spy. He also killed his *Muslim* servant for no reason. He was resting in the rest area and told his servant to roast the meat. The servant was also tired, so he fell asleep as well. Then, when *Abdullah* woke up and he saw him sleeping he killed him. So, he was wanted in that blood also. *Fartanah* accepted *Islam* while *Qareebah* was killed.

Huwairith was not only spreading derogatory words, but he was with *Habbar Ibnul Aswad* when they made the camel of *Zainab*, the daughter of the *Prophet* to run when she was migrating to *Medina*. She fell on her belly, she lost her baby and became sick and later died. So, they were both wanted in two bloods. But *Habbar* came to the *Prophet* proclaiming *Shahadah* from far and held of the hand of *Prophet*, so the *Prophet* pardoned him.

Miqyas Ibni Dubabah had already accepted *Islam*. His brother *Hisham* was killed by a *Muslim* in the battle by mistake and even though this *Miqyas* received the blood money, he killed that *Muslim*, so he was declared to be a killer and *Numailah* killed him in *Qisas*. *Abdullah Ibni Abi Sarah* was pardoned by *Uthman* as they were both milk brothers. This *Abdullah* accepted *Islam*, but then denounced it, so he was declared to be a wanted man. When he apologized wholeheartedly, he was pardoned by the *Prophet*. He remained a sincere *Muslim* and became a great general of *Islam* after that. He passed away in *Sajdah* in *Fajr* prayers as he used to always pray,

> "O Allah! Cause my death in a closer form of mine to you.
> Fajr prayer and then the form of Sajdah!"

- *Ikramah Ibni Abi Jah'l* got pardoned by his wife, *Umm Hakim*, since she approached the *Prophet*. This was the only one who attacked the *Muslim* army when they were marching in the outskirts of *Makkah*.

- *Kab Ibni Zuhair*, a poet and from a poet family, used to say bad things about *Islam* but got pardoned by the *Prophet*.

- *Harith Ibni Hisham* and *Zuhair Ibni Umayyah* got shelter in the house of *Ummi Hani*, the sister of *Ali* as she was married to someone in their family. *Ali* was standing at the door outside to get them and kill them. *Ummi Hani* shouted to the *Prophet* of *Allah* that she has sheltered these two men, but my brother wants to kill them. *Prophet* said,

> "We shelter whom you sheltered",

So, *Ali* came back and here jurists got a point that a *Muslim* woman can shelter someone as well and that shelter may be honored.

- *Safwan Ibni Umayyah* was the son of *Umayyah Ibni Khalaf*, the arch enemy of the *Prophet*. He used to torture *Bilal* physically and *Prophet* mentally. His son was going in his footsteps. But when his first cousin, *Umair Ibni Wahab* approached the *Prophet* saying that you have announced a general amnesty, so please if you can withdraw your declaration about *Safwan*. *Prophet* accepted it. He said, but being a very sensitive man, he will not believe me, so if you can give me some sign as a surety for him that I am not trapping him. *Prophet* gave him his turban, so he came back and asked the *Prophet* to give him some time to think on whether he would accept *Islam* or not. The *Prophet* agreed to it. After the conquest of *Makkah*, when the *Prophet* was informed that the people of *Taif* were making some arrangements to attack *Muslims* he planned to go in that direction to counter that uprising. He asked *Safwan* for 40,000 *Dirham* and the steel jackets he had. He said, by force!

The *Prophet* said,

"*No, but borrow.*"

So, he gave it to the *Prophet* and he joined the expedition, even though he had not yet accepted *Islam*. After that the battle was over the *Prophet* gave him 300 camels from the booty, but still he was looking at a bigger bunch of booty.

The *Prophet* said,

"*You like it?*"

He said, of course. The *Prophet* said, then take it. He took it and said that kings do not give like this, but only a Messenger. So, he accepted *Islam*.

- *Wahshi Ibni Harb* is the one who cleft the chest of *Hamzah*, the uncle of *Prophet*, in the battle of *Uhud* and amputated his organs, which caused the *Prophet* to break into tears when he saw this type of insult and cruelty to a dead body. But this *Wahshi* who was declared to be wanted because of that war crime went to the *Prophet* and accepted *Islam*, and the *Prophet* pardoned him. *Hind*, the daughter of *Otbah* who hired this *Wahshi* for that job, also came and accepted *Islam*, so the *Prophet* pardoned her too. So, out of those fifteen people, only four were killed.

Now, the point is that the cause of *Jihad* is *Harabah*, the imposition of war in one way or the other and not *Kufr* or *Shirk*.

HARABAH

OPINION OF JURISTS AND WARS OF THE *PROPHET*

As we mentioned earlier, the cause for *Jihad* according to all schools is *Harabah*. This term is short but more inclusive than *Harb* which means war. But *Harabah* means war, to plot and plan a war, conspiracy, and oppression, so we can use the term *Zulm* (injustice) for these aforesaid meanings. What was the case in the times of *Prophet*? His wars were defense or offense also. So, some scholars said, sometimes it was offense also, while a vast majority of them say, it was defense even though if it seemed like an offense in certain cases. The first group presented the battle of *Banu Mustalaq*, *Khaybar* and *Muta* as offensive wars where the *Prophet* took or sent his army to those areas to fight, but when we study the situation and background in depth, we find that these battles were also fought in defense.

The *Prophet* was informed that *Banu Mustalaq* tribe was planning under the leadership of its leader *Harith Ibni Abi Darrar* to attack *Muslims*, so *Prophet* dispatched an army in *Shaban* of the sixth *Hijri* against them. In this battle the whole tribe of *Banu Mustalaq* was captured as prisoners of war. Only ten people were killed. The daughter of their king named *Jawairiyah* offered herself for marriage to the *Prophet*. The *Prophet* accepted it with the leave of *Allah*. Then companions of the *Prophet* suggested that these prisoners could be released since they all became his in-laws.

Regarding the battle of *Khaybar*, the *Prophet* received the news that the Jews of *Khaybar* and *Ghitfan* tribe had a secret treaty to launch a mission against *Muslims*. *Prophet* sent an army that reached the valley of *Rajee* in between *Ghitfan* and *Khaybar* to cut off their link and captured the area. Still, he spared them to remain in their land to do farming and to pay a portion of the product to the state.

While *Muta* appears as an offensive move, but has features of defense as people of the area killed 15 people who were there as missionaries to convey the Message. *Prophet* sent a message to the chief of *Basrah Sharahbeel Ibni Amr*. He killed the messenger. So, *Prophet* sent an army consisting of three thousand *Muslims*. *Sharahbeel* faced them with one hundred thousand soldiers, but *Muslims* defeated them. The next year Caesar arranged a big army in the same area of *Muta* for revenge. *Prophet* arranged 30,000 *Muslims* to march towards *Tabuk* who stayed there for 20 days but Caesar retreated and did not face *Muslims*.

Now-a-days this is called an offensive move. So, even though the cause of *Jihad* is *Harabah*, *Prophet* mostly launched defensive moves. But offensive war is also allowed. However, it depends on the circumstances because when in the *Battle of Trench* after a besiege of almost one month or so, the allied forces withdrew as frustrated losers, the *Prophet* said to his *Sahabahs* (companions)

> *"Now the Quraysh will never attack you after this, but you will."*

This means *Muslim* offensive is allowed. Then, *Prophet* attacked *Makkah* to recapture his own homeland from where *Muslims* were driven out for no reason. We can say that his defensive war was regarding actual attack when he was attacked, while his offensive moves were also defensive. But for other types of injustice like conspiracy to counter it or help *Muslims* under oppression when they cry for help or to counter other types of *Fitnah*, since *Fitnahi* is of various types.

PRE-EMPTIVE WAR

The conspiracy and *Fitnah* is known to rulers and people in authority, so they must decide. Sometimes when they launch a war which looks like an offense but, in fact, that is a defense, which is launched as a precaution.

DEFENSE

As we mentioned before, defense is not only a right but a duty as well, and if one can defend and he does not then that is a sin in *Islam*. This defense is of two types:

i. Private Defense

ii. Public Defense

For private defense we would like to present the story of the two sons of *Adam, Habil* and *Qabil*.

Verse 5:27-31 of the *Holy Qur'an* says,

> *"And recite to them the story of Adam's two sons when they both offered a sacrifice each, and it was accepted from one of them (Habil) but it was not accepted from the other. The latter said, I will surely, kill you. Said (former), "Verily, Allah accepts from the pious people (and if you raise your hand against me to kill me, I shall not raise my hand to kill you. Verily, I fear Allah, the Lord*

of Worlds. Indeed, I want you to have my sin and your sin as well, so you may be of the companions of Fire and that is the recompense of wrongdoers. So, he himself permitted (made easy) for him the killing of his brother. So, he killed him (his brother) and became one of the losers. Then, Allah sent a raven scratching the ground to show him, how to hide the dead body of his brother. He said, "O woe to me! Have I failed to be like this raven and hide the dead body of my brother, and he was full of regrets."

Now, one application of verse 5:30 is that *Habil* became a loser as he lost his life, since he made his murder easy for his brother as he did not defend himself, which was his duty.

And in the case of public defense we would like to mention the story of *Bani Israel* as they did not defend themselves against their enemies, so they lost everything including their homes, properties, and their families, even their honor and dignity. So sometime later they came to their *Prophet* at the time, *Samuel*, as *Allah* narrated the story.

Verse 2:246 says,

"Have you not seen (learnt from the story of) the Children of Israel after Moses when they said to their prophet, "Appoint for us a king, so we may fight in the path of Allah. He said, "What if you decline to fight the fight when it is made incumbent upon you?" They said, "What! Why would we not fight in the path of Allah while we have been driven out of our homes, and (deprived) of our children so when the fight was prescribed for them they turned away except only a few of them."

These fewer people fought wholeheartedly to fulfill their obligation and to perform their duty. Thus, *Allah* gave them victory over their enemies.

There is another story of *Bani Israel* (*Children of Israel*) that when *Pharaoh* was drowned, *Allah* ordered *Musa* (*Moses*) to take them to their own land, the *Holy Land*. But they refused to go.

In verses 5:21-26 *Allah* says,

> *"(Musa (as) said), O my people! Enter the Holy Land which Allah has assigned to you and do not turn away (from fighting as that is your duty), otherwise, you will be losers." They said, "O Musa! There is a nation of tyrannical strength (fighters) and we will never enter therein, until they leave it. If they will go out of there, then we will enter." Two men from those who feared whom Allah had bestowed favor, said, "Enter upon them through the gate and when you have entered then you will prevail, and rely upon Allah if you are believers." They said, "O Musa! We will never enter there as long as they are there, so go, you and your Lord (means your big brother, Harun) and fight. We are sitting here." He said, "O my Lord, I do not own but myself and my brother, so part us from the defiantly disobedient people. He (Allah) said, "Then this (land) is forbidden for them for forty years. They will wander throughout the land (of Sinai desert). So, do not grieve over the defiantly disobedient people."*

They did not fulfill their obligation and duty, so they got into the difficulty of wandering. Yes, there was wisdom in it that most of these mentally enslaved people died during these forty years and a new generation was developed in a natural but difficult atmosphere, and then they entered the *Holy Land* with *Prophet Yusha*.

Regardless, in the case of personal defense everyone decides for himself for what to do and how to do it.

The *Prophet* said,

> *"Whosoever got killed to defend his life or his property or his honor or his faith, he is a "Shaheed" (martyred)."*

But in the case of public defense, one case is that of the protection of the society. If someone is going to harm the society, the society itself or through the authority is bound to stop, control, or counter him in any possible way. But in case if the society is attacked by the enemy, now basically that is the duty of the state to defend and to declare a countering and defensive war.

BUT IF IT DOES NOT, THEN WHAT?

There is one *Shar'ee* Maxim.

> *"La Qitala illa Bil Imam"* – No fight but with *"Imam"* (Leader or *"Khalifa"*, an Islamic title).

One of the required qualities of *Imam* in *Islam* is that he has the power to address any fear and danger and to defend the state and the people therein, their lives, their properties, their honors, and their faith and religion. If he does not, he does not perform his duties and does not fulfill his obligations. If he could not, then he is losing his authority or even lost it, so if someone else from his people will not come forward to take the responsibility and to defend the state, it will fall to the enemies. That's why *Sharia* says, when the enemy forces entered the state land, then *Jihad*, which is a *Fardi-Kifayah* i.e., collective responsibility to defend and that's why in such a situation, a woman will come out to fight without the permission of her husband and a son will come out without the permission of his father. So, in such a situation an *Imam* is not going to declare *Jihad* he loses his status as

> *"La Imama illa Bil Qital"* – *no ruler without a will to fight.*

So, if he does not fulfill his obligation, naturally people will take it into their hands as they will not look at the enemy killing them, looting their properties or their honors and dignity. So, to defend the state that is a duty, but a much more important duty because the citizens are protected if the state is protected.

DARUL ISLAM

The jurists have defined it in different ways but the common concept of an *Islamic* state is where the *Muslims* have their own sovereignty over a land that everyone can practice openly the rules of *Islam* and keeps its signs and symbols and the rulers can implement its rules and laws. It means that there is a piece of land with *Muslims* in majority ruled by *Muslim* rulers freely and with sovereignty means they have their own system of government and their own army to maintain it and to defend it.

Now, when there is a state like this, the citizens, even if they are non-*Muslim Zimmis* protected citizens, it is a must to defend it. Also, this is incumbent upon its rulers to implement *Islamic* rules and laws therein.

COULD *DARUL ISLAM* BE CONVERTED TO *DARUL KUFR* AGAIN?

Jumhur means three *Imams* i.e., *Malik, Shafi'* and *Ahmad* said when a state got declared *Darul Islam* it could never be converted as *Darul*

Kufr again, even though the non-*Muslim* population overtook it and declared it as their state or a part of their state. So, according to them, this is incumbent upon *Muslims* to recapture it at any price. *Abu Hanifa* and his followers say, we must look at the facts that when it has been overtaken by non-*Muslims*, merged to their state or declared as their state, then its status got changed as well from *Darul Islam* to *Darul Kufr*, but it has a few conditions:

i. That is adjacent to *Darul Kufr*;

ii. Those who overtook it implemented their rules there openly;

iii. No *Muslim* or even non-*Muslim* citizens of the previous *Islamic* state live there. It is still based on his old status but he got a new status and a new pledge.

For *Darul Islam* to be *Darul Islam* it is enough that the ruler can implement the *Sharia* laws, but if not yet implemented there, that is still *Darul Islam* and an *Islamic* state - yes, the rule is a sinner if he has not implemented ... not *Islamic* laws. Unfortunately, some emotional *Muslims* are of the view that when laws of *Islam* are not implemented, the state can be a *Muslim* once but not an *Islamic* one.

SPOILS OF WAR

Another issue is the Booty or Spoils of War when *Muslims* get and avail some booty in the battle they own it collectively. When they saved it, and preserved it by bringing it to their state, which means inside their boundaries as its ownership depends on it, one-fifth of that will go to those mentioned in

Ayah 8:41 of *Surat Ul Anfal*,

> *"And know that whatever you obtained of the War Booty then, indeed, for Allah is its one-fifth and for the Messenger, for his near relatives, for orphans, the poor and travelers."*

The name of *Allah* is mentioned here, not for a share but for blessing, or that this is by His order. So, this one-fifth will go to these five people and the remaining would be distributed to the soldiers in that war. But what if the enemy got ahold of the *Muslim* wealth in the battlefield? Do they own it?

Again, this is a disputed issue. *Malik, Shafi,* and *Ahmad* said that they do not own it. So, if anything is found later in their land by *Muslims* it will go to its original *Muslim* owner as it has never gone out of his ownership under *Islamic* rules.

They based their saying on verse 4:141 of the *Holy Qur'an* which says,

> "And Allah will never give to disbelievers a way over the believers."

So, by giving them ownership we give them a way over the believers. *Imam Abu Hanifa* says that, ideologically, this is right but practically and physically they owned it. These are the facts of ground, so if something of that is later found by the *Muslims* in their land, so if that is not brought to the *Muslims* land, the very owner can take it. But when it got to the *Muslim* land then it is part of the Booty, a collective right of the *Muslim* fighters. The original owner can take it for a reasonable price and that price will go to the booty.

Abu Hanifa referred to *Ayah* 59:8 of *Surat Ul Hashr*,

> "The Fay received by Muslims from their enemies without war) is for the poor emigrants, who have been driven out of their homes and their properties, seeking the bounty of Allah and His good pleasure and help Allah and His Messenger. They are the truthful."

In this verse *Allah* called them *Fuqara*, which means having no wealth even though *Allah* has attributed to them their homes and properties. But as their enemies possessed that, so they are called *Fuqara*, which means that the enemies got the ownership, otherwise, if still that belongs to these *Muslims*, then how they are called *Fuqara* (the poor).

CEASEFIRE

We have already said that in *Islam* to start and launch a war is very difficult as it requires that certain conditions and pre-requisites are fulfilled. But when it is started and launched in accordance with *Qur'an* and *Sunnah*, then to stop it is also difficult because:

i. It is not acceptable for *Muslims* to ask for ceasefire in normal circumstances.

   Allah said,

   "So, do not be weak and do not call for peace as you are high and Allah is with you and He will never deprive you of your deeds."

"You are high" means in faith and belief, so do not lower the position of your true faith or you will either get a victory, and that is a high status in the world, or you will get martyred in the path of *Allah* and that is also a high status in the Hereafter, or fighting itself in the cause of

Allah is high besides victory and martyrdom as *Allah* is with you and you will have the reward of your deeds anyway.

ii. You started the fight to counter cruelty, brutality, conspiracy, or *Fitnah* and in verse 2:193 *Allah* says,

> "And fight them until no "Fitnah" remains there and "Deen" to be that of Allah."

iii. You have not imposed war but you do counter it and in verse 2:194 *Allah* says,

> "So whoever assaults you, then assault him in the same way."

iv. A *Hadith* by *Ibni Umar* says that the *Prophet* said,

> "I have been ordered to fight people till they say that there is no god but Allah and Muhammad is the Messenger of Allah."

Thus, the fight should be waged until they say *Shahadah* or ask for peace in one way or the other as in verse 8:61 *Allah* says,

> "And if they incline to peace, then you incline to it as well and rely upon Allah. Verily, He is All-Hearing, All-Knowing."

In *Islam* there is no coercion to convert someone.

The verse 2:256 of *Holy Qur'an* says,

> "There is no coercion in "Deen" (to convert someone by force)."

Yet someone said *Shahadah* because of fear to himself, it is accepted because one becomes *Muslim* by tongue. What is in the heart it is known to *Allah* alone, so the *Prophet* became angry with *Osamah Ibni Zaid* when he said that he killed that one who said *Shahadah* because he said it only to protect himself and not from his heart or didn't know he said it from heart, so, the *Prophet* said then

"why you did not cleave his heart?"

So, for one to stop the war on him is when he said *Shahadah*. The other reason is, if someone asked for shelter, it means he threw his weapon, raised his hands and asked for shelter.

In verse 9:6 *Allah* says,

"And if anyone of the polytheists asked for a shelter from you, then shelter him."

And even if that shelter is given to someone by a common *Muslim*, not a big general, still that is to be honored as the *Prophet* said,

"The" Zimmah" of Muslims is one of their lowest one, even.... can play it."

While *Zimmah* means responsibility, here it means the promise, the treaty, which means that when one *Muslim* promised shelter to someone then all *Muslims* must honor that, otherwise they will lose their credibility and no one will trust their promises, even if a non-combatant *Muslim* such as a woman promises the same to someone, that may be honored as well. But the situation and circumstances may be taken into consideration as the *Prophet* of *Allah* said to *Ummi Hani*,

"We shelter whom you sheltered."

Also, when the daughter of the *Prophet*, *Zainab*, sheltered her husband *Abul Aas*, the *Prophet* honored that. The reason is well known: even a non-practicing *Muslim* does not compromise in matters of *Deen* and does not want to harm it, rather he thinks of what is best for *Deen* and that's why circumstances may be considered.

The *Malikites* say that in the case of shelter everything must be made clear that this is only for this person or his family, but other three *Imams* said that shelter to a person includes his family and his belongings as well so no *Jizyah* may be assessed on them. Later on, if it was conceived of them that under the cover of this shelter they are doing some conspiracy or they try to create a *Fitnah*, then according to *Hanafites* the *Imam* will denounce that shelter. But the other three schools of jurisprudence are of the view that shelter treaty is a binding treaty, so if they have not done something practical it cannot be dropped and denounced. But we say that this is totally in the hands of *Imam* and authorities, as they look at it in a broader sense. Without denouncing it openly, they may not be killed or attacked. *Mua'wiyah* had a treaty of no war with Romans for an appointed period. When it was close to being lapsed, *Mua'wiyah* started to take his army towards their boundaries to attack them as soon as the period ended. Suddenly, some dust was seen and someone riding a fast running horse was seen shouting at the top of his voice, *Wafa'um La Ghadrun*. When he came, he was a companion of the *Prophet*, *Amr Ibni Anbasah*. He told *Mua'wiyah* that the *Prophet* said when you are not going to renew the treaty then you must tell them before the lapse of the period of treaty.

Verse 8:58 of the *Holy Qur'an* says,

> *"And if you have fear from a people then throw back to them (their treaty) on equal terms. Verily, Allah does not like traitors."*

MUSTAMIN

When a non-*Muslim* from outside has permission to enter an *Islamic* state then under normal circumstances he can go anywhere in the state. But if the rules are other way around, he can enter *Makkah* and stay there for only three days and nights according to *Abu Hanifa*. *Imam Malik* says he can stay there for three days and nights, but he cannot enter the *Masjidul Haram*, while according to Shafiites and *Hanbalis* they cannot enter the vicinity of *Haram* and the land of *Hijaz* as Umar said,

> *"If I am still alive I will take them out of the Peninsula."*

Later, he left them in *Yemen*, which is a part of Peninsula, so that's why they say, *"by Jazeera,"* he meant the land of *Hijaz*. But again, it depends on the situation and *Imam* can decide accordingly. All these *Imams* referred to verse 9:28,

> *"O you who believe! Indeed, the polytheists are unclean, so let them not approach the al-Masjidul Haram after this year."*

So, *Shafiites* and *Hanbalis* said, no approach to the *Masjidul Haram* means the land of *Haram*. *Imam Malik* said that the actual *Masjid* is forbidden for them while *Imam Abu Hanifa* said that this verse and from verses 1-33 that *Ali* recited at the time of *Hajj* under the leadership of *Abu Bakr* one year before the *Hajj* of *Prophet* that at that time polytheists were in *Hajj* as well and they used to do their *Tawaf* naked, clapping and whistling in *Tawaf*. So, when he recited these verses then *Abu Bakr* announced and declared that

> *"No polytheist is allowed to do Hajj after this (year), nor any naked (person), can do "Tawaf" of the House of Allah."*

So, *Abu Hanifa* said, expressly this verse is regarding *Hajj* and *Tawaf*, but implicitly regarding their stay in *Makkah* for more than three days and nights – but still it depends as their entrance in *Makkah* depends on permission as every state has some restricted or prohibited areas. So, this is the restricted area by *Allah* and as someone can enter that restricted area with permission, same is the case here.

HUDNAH (TRUCE)

Literally, *Hudnah* means suspension of hostilities between the belligerents. In *Sharia* it means a peace treaty for an appointed period. This could be made by the head of state or his assistant, for free or for money. The *Hanafites* are of the view that if a group of *Muslims* did the same, and the good of the *Islamic* state is obvious, it is also acceptable. The *Imam* will approve that and ultimately it becomes a treaty by the *Imam*.

In verses 8:61-62 *Allah* says,

> *"If they are inclined towards a peace treaty then you may be inclined to that also, and place your trust in Allah. Verily, He is All-Hearing, All-Knowing. And if they intend to deceive you (in this regard) then sufficient for you is Allah. It is He Who supported you with his help and with believers."*

Also, in verse 9:7 *Allah* says,

"So, as long as they are upright towards you (in keeping up the promise) be upright towards them. Verily, Allah loves the righteous (who keep their word)."

The Jews of Banu Nadeer were under the treaty of Medina, but when they asked the Prophet to come to their area to resolve a problem, they plotted to assassinate the Prophet, but Prophet saw, as one person was there on the top of the wall who was appointed to throw a big rock on the Prophet. So, the Prophet terminated their treaty and protection, and expelled them to Khaybar. (Bayhaqi)

The *Hanafites* and *Malikites* are of the view that this is for the *Imam* to determine the time limit while *Imam Ahmed* said that this is acceptable up to ten years as the pact of *Hudaibiyah* by the *Prophet* with the people of *Makkah* was for ten years and *Shafiites* said that if *Muslims* are weak then it could be up to ten years, otherwise it could be from four months to less than one year.

ZIMMAH AND *JIZYAH*

Literally, *Zimmah* means conscious, moral sense, security, covenant, and *Jizyah* means tribute or tax on a tributary. *Zimmah* and *Jizyah* are linked to each other in this sense, as the *Zimmah* means a contract or pledge of non-*Muslims* to an *Islamic* state by paying a specific amount annually to the state to avail their rights of citizenship. As this is a contract with the state, the *Imam* or his assistant can and do approve it. *Imam Malik* said, any *Muslim* can give this right to a non-*Muslim* but later it may be approved by the state. Now there is a specific department for this purpose with its own rules and procedures that are different in different countries. The *Imam* can take this right back based on some solid grounds, but it will require taking the person back to his or her secure place as in verse 9:6 *Allah* said,

> *"And if one from the polytheists asked your protection then grant him protection, so he may hear the words of Allah then deliver him to his place of safety."*

If some non-*Muslim* comes to an *Islamic* state on temporary basis and then asks for permanent residence as *Zimmi*, a protected citizen, the *Islamic* state can consider his application.

CONDITIONS FOR *ZIMMAH*

In verse 9:29 *Allah* says,

> *"Fight those who do not believe in Allah or in the Last Day and (they) do not consider unlawful what Allah and his Messenger have made unlawful and do not adopt the religion of Truth from those who were given the Scripture, until they give "Jizyah" willingly while they are humbled."*

Most of the scholars limited this concept of *Jizyah* and *Zimmah* to the *People of the Book* as that is in the text, but *Imam Abu Hanifa, Shafi'* and *Ahmad* extended this rule to *Magians* (*Majus*) as *Imam Malik* narrated a *Hadith* that *Umar*, the second *Caliph*, said,

> *"I don't know what is to be done to them, so Abdur Rahman Ibni Auf said, "I testify that the Prophet said, "Deal with them like that of the People of the Book. (Mu'atta)"*

Also, *Ahmad, Bukhari, Abu Dawud* and *Tirmizi* narrated from *Abdur Rahman Ibni Auf* that the *Prophet* took *Jizyah* from the *Magians* of *Hajar*.

Imam Malik Auza'ee, Thauri and other jurists of *Sham* (Syria) included this rule of *Jizyah* to all non-*Muslims* as *Imam Muslim* narrates from *Buraidah* that whenever the Messenger of *Allah* was appointing someone as a leader of the army or expedition, he used to enjoin him to fear *Allah* and to be good to his fellow *Muslims*, He used to tell him,

> "When you encounter your enemy then call him towards Islam and if they refuse then ask them to accept "Jizyah.""

Now, here the *Prophet* did not specify the enemy, but mentioned them in general. So, this rule generally applies to all non-*Muslims*.

The other condition is that this treaty could not be signed with those who denounced *Islam* after they accepted *Islam* because the apostate (*Murtad*) has to enter the fold of *Islam* or his case of apostasy may be taken to the court and he would be executed.

The *Prophet* said,

> "Whosoever changed his "Deen" (of Islam), kill him (Bukhari, Abu Dawud, Tirmizi, Nisa'i, Ibni Majah)."

This is because *Islam* is the foundation of the *Islamic* state and its ideology and its constitution, so the one who denounced it commits high treason, so his case may be proceeded in the court of law (constitutional court).

Thirdly, *Zimmah* treaty is not time-bound because this is a substitute for *Islam* as far as protection is concerned.

JIZYAH BUT FOR WHO?

The next issue is what type of person is eligible for *Jizyah*?

The *Jizyah* would be assessed for one –

i. Who is sane and adult; there may not be any *Jizyah* for an insane or minor because they are non-combatant.

ii. *Jizyah* would be imposed on men, not women, as they are neither combatant, nor bound to work and earn.

In verse 9:29 *Allah* says,

"Fight those who did not believe."

And fighters are only sane and adult men.

iii. *Jizyah* may be imposed on one who is healthy and earning. There is no *Jizyah* on one who is either permanently sick or does not earn his living. There may not be any *Jizyah* on a too-old person or a blind or crippled person, and same is the case of those who have devoted themselves to volunteer for the religious activities. This is the *Madhab* of *Hanafites* and *Malikites*. *Shafiites* and *Hanbalis* do not drop the *Jizyah* for certain excuses, but minors, women, insane, paralyzed, the blind and the too old are not bound to pay *Jizyah*. *Ali* said whosoever has our *Zimmah* treaty, their blood is like our blood and his wealth is like our wealth, meaning secure (*Dari Qutni*). In other words, he said that they are giving *Jizyah*, so their wealth may be like our wealth (meaning secure).

Osamah relates from the Prophet that he said whosoever did injustice to a Zimmi (the protected citizen) or caused him some harm or over-burdened him or took something of him without his consent, then I will be a pleader for him (Ahmad, Abu Dawud, Bayhaqi).

TYPES OF *JIZYAH*

Jizyah is of two types:

i) *Jizyah* by consent – when some non-*Muslim* asked for peace and protection, that they shall pay to the *Islamic* state for this purpose.

ii) *Jizyah* by force – when *Muslims* overtake an area and impose *Jizyah* on non-*Muslims* there and leave them, along with their belongings, that the state will protect them and their properties.

RATIO OF *JIZYAH*

Hanafites and *Hanbalis* say that a rich man having ten thousand *Dirham* will pay 48 *Dirham* per year i.e., four *Dirham* every month.

A medium one who has two hundred *Dirham* will pay 24 *Dirham* annually, but in installments i.e., two *Dirham* per month and an earning hand will pay 12 *Dirham* per year i.e., one *Dirham* every month. This is according to what *Umar* did in *Iraq*.

Malikites say that whoever has gold will pay four *Dinar* per year while the one who has silver will pay 40 *Dirham* annually. The ratio may not be increased for a rich person, only a poor one. *Imam Shafi'* said that minimum *Jizyah* per year will be one *Dinar* as the *Prophet* said to *Muaaz Ibni Jabal* when he was sending him to *Yemen* to take one *Dinar* from every adult person or *Yemeni* fabric equal to that. Two *Dinars* may be taken from a medium-rich person according to *Imam Shafi'* as *Umar* did so, and from a rich person, 4 *Dinars* per year.

This payment may be made in the beginning of every year or month according to *Hanafites* as he is paying security for himself. But *Jumhur* said they will pay that at the end of the year as they are paying for the security they already availed.

This contract is binding on the state, so the state cannot dissolve it one sided unless for a solid reason, while from the *Zimmi* side this is not binding, meaning that if they want they can drop it and they may be taken out to the boundaries of a non-*Muslim* state safely as they don't want to be the protected citizens of the *Islamic* state anymore. But this is practical only if they have migrated from a non-*Muslim* state that is their birth place or if a non-*Muslim* state is ready to accept them, because the political situation now-a-days has changed a lot and almost everything is documented and bounded.

This contract gets dropped according to *Hanafites* in the following three situations:

i. When a *Zimmi* accepted *Islam*. So, he is not required to pay *Jizyah* anymore as *Muslims* do not pay it to the *Islamic* state.

ii. The *Zimmi* migrated to *Darul Harb* and got settled there then the *Islamic* state is not responsible for him anymore.

iii. The *Zimmis* stood up against the state, started fighting, and overtook an area, so now there is a fight, thus no protection. So, the *Zimmah* contract automatically drops by itself.

All other actions do not drop this contract, like if a *Zimmi* killed a *Muslim* unjustly, or he committed *Zina* (rape, adultery or fornication) with a *Muslim* woman or even if he used a bad word against *Islam* and the *Prophet* of *Islam*, or he refused to pay *Jizyah*. In such cases the state must take *Jizyah* from them. All other things are less than disbelief and we are taking *Jizyah* from them along with their disbelief. Crimes are to be dealt with separately according to the law.

But the other three *Imams, Malik, Shafi'* and *Ahmad* said that when they refuse to pay *Jizyah* or they refuse the application of public laws on them or get together to fight against *Muslims* then their contract of *Zimmah* is no more intact because all these things are the requirements of that contract. *Imam Shafi* said that the contract stands dissolved if these actions are mentioned there in the contract as binding.

So, according to all schools the pledge of allegiance to the state means subjugating himself to civil and criminal laws of the land because public laws could not be of more than one type. Certain things are considered as private or personal laws like their own ways of marriage, divorce, inheritance, or their own ways of worship and even drinking wine or eating pork, so they may be left alone with these practices of them as the *Prophet* said,

> "*Leave them alone and their religious practices.*"

As we said before, according to *Hanafites, Jizyah* may be taken at the beginning of the year, while according to the other three *Imams* it is at the end of the year, and it gets dropped with the acceptance of *Islam* as *Ibni Umar* said that for whosoever accepted *Islam* there is no *Jizyah* on him (*Tabarani*).

It also gets dropped with the death of a *Zimmi* according to *Hanafites* and *Malikites*, while according to *Shafiites* and *Hanbalis* when the year or a part of the year has passed then *Jizyah* was due on him which he has not paid, so that may be taken from his property. The reason according to *Hanafites* is that *Jizyah* was supposed to have been taken at the start of the year and since it was not taken, it gets dropped, while according to *Malikites* even though the year has passed and he was supposed to pay, he did not and he died, so now the death demolished it.

Abu Hanifa said that even if he is alive and the *Jizyah* has not been taken and the year has passed and a new year started, so the past year dues are dropped to not over-burden him and this *Jizyah* resembles a fixed punishment for crimes and in more than one-time crime of the similar nature there is only one punishment. That is called *Tadakhul* (intermeddling).

RIGHTS AND DUTIES OF *ZIMMIS*

Like all other contracts this *Zimmah* contract also determines some rights and duties.

RIGHTS OF *ZIMMIS*

The rights of *Zimmis* are as follows:

A. A *Zimmi* can move in the *Islamic* state anywhere freely. The only thing is that they cannot live inside the land of *Haram* since in verse 9:28 *Allah* says,

> *"O you who believed! Indeed, the polytheists are unclean, so let them not approach the al-Masjidul Haram after this year of them."*

Now, based on this verse, *Imam Shafi* says that a non-*Muslim* cannot enter the land of *Haram* and the whole of *Hijaz* area as well, as *Umar* said,

"If I am alive I will turn them out of Jazeeratul Arab,"

But as he left them in *Yemen*, only *Hijaz* remains there. He said that if he gained entry secretly, he may be turned out therefrom and if is he died and buried there, so as long as body is not rotten and decomposed, it may be taken out and buried outside.

Imam Ahmad said that they could be allowed into the land of *Hijaz* for trade only for three days, but not in the land of *Haram*. The *Malikites* allowed them to live in the *Jazeeratul Arab*, which means *Hijaz* and Yemen both. They are also allowed their entry to the land of *Haram*, but not to the *Masjid-Ul-Haram*, while *Imam Abu Hanifa* says, they cannot live inside the land of *Haram*. Their entry to the land of *Haram* is allowed.

Note: The land of *Haram* was marked for the first time by *Prophet Ibrahim* (Abraham) based on the revelation. Then the *Prophet* renewed it and now it is very well known and even documented. From all directions the signboards make it very clear.

B. Their lives, properties, honors, etc., are safe and secure;

C. They would be left free with their worship places, ways of worship, and their personal and private laws. They can keep swine but they can neither drink in public, nor can they bring their swine to the public *Bazars*. If they did, they would be disciplined by some punishment.

DUTIES OF *ZIMMIS*

Their duties are as follows:

i. Everyone who is bound to pay *Jizyah* will pay *Jizyah* only once a year.

ii. If a *Muslim* is passing by his specific town and wants to stay there, they will provide him boarding, lodging for three days and nights.

iii. Whatever trade they do outside their country, they will pay one-tenth of that to the state;

iv. They will not open any new worship place in a city of *Muslims* only;

v. They will not use rides of such type that show their pomp;

vi. They should have some visible identity so that they are not bothered for things they are not bound to do like prayer at prayer times because in an *Islamic* state the *Muslims* are to be ordered for prayer at prayer times.

vii. They will not shelter any spy or outsider without bringing it to the notice of authorities because it may be that the outsider is dangerous to the state and that even *Zimmi* does not know.

viii. They will not stop *Muslims* if they want to visit their worship places.

ix. They will respect *Muslims* and their religion.

x. They will not display their religious signs openly.

xi. They will not use any bad words or show insult to any *Prophet* or the *Prophet* of *Islam*.

AHADITH ABOUT *ZIMMIS*

Ibni Umar narrated that in the time of Prophet one Muslim killed a "Zimmi." The Prophet ordered his retribution and said, "I am much more responsible than who fulfills his obligation (Dari Qutni)."

Umar Ibnul Khattab in his time when a *Muslim* from *Bakr Ibni Wa'il* tribe killed a *Zimmi* handed him over to his son-in-law and he killed him as retribution. One *Muslim* was charged for the killing of a *Zimmi*. *Ali* ordered his *Qisas* (retribution), but the brother of the *Zimmi* came saying that I have forgiven him. He said maybe he has threatened you?

He said,

"No, but he has given me the blood-money."

Regarding *Zimmis* and their responsibilities *Umar* said that they may not be overburdened and *Ali* said that for the payment of their dues neither their donkey be sold, nor their cows, nor their dress. Also for injustice to them one would be fired and disciplined. *Imam Abu Yusuf* writes in his book *Kifabul Kharaj* that *Umar* wrote to his governor in *Sham*, *Abu Ubaidah*, to forbid *Muslims* not to do any injustice to them or harm them or gobble their properties.

Also, when he saw a collector punishing *Zimmis*, *Umar* said,

> *"Do not punish them as those who punish others in this world, Allah will punish them in the Hereafter."*

He saw an old man begging, so he asked him why? He said,

> *"I am too old to earn and to pay the "Jizyah."*

He brought him to his secretary of exchequer and said to drop the *Jizyah* and to help him continuously.

His wording at that time was:

> *"This is not justice that we have eaten his youth (earnings) and then we humiliate him when he is old."*

Khalid Ibnul Waleed wrote to the people of *Heerah* that he has decided that anyone of them who cannot work or some sickness befallen him or he was rich and became poor and his people are supporting him now, his *Jizyah* is dropped and he may be given welfare from the national exchequer for him and his family.

Bayhaqi narrates that the Christians of *Banu Taghlib* tribe asked *Umar*,

> *"If you can please change the title of "Jizyah" for what you are taking from us, so please take it in the name of "Zakat" or charity that you take from Muslims in that name. He said, but that is their worship title. They asked*

if there was any other title? Umar said give it any title they wanted."

All jurists say that this is permissible.

PRISONERS OF WAR

As it is a well-known in *Islam* that the killing of people is not meant in *Qital* (battle), but it happens as candies are not getting distributed in battles. If someone surrenders, he may not be killed but only captured as a prisoner of war. Before *Islam*, in almost every culture they used to kill the captives or to make them their slaves forever. Sometimes in abnormal situations some killing is needed, but that is not the basic philosophy of *Islam* as in verse 21:107 *Allah* said regarding *Prophet Muhammed*,

"And We have not sent you but a (perfect) mercy for the worlds."

And *Prophet* said,

"I am a gifted (or a guided) Mercy."

His Message and the Message of all messengers was

"La Ilaha Ilallah"

meaning there is no god (worthy of worship and ruler) but only *Allah* which means that the Lord is only *Allah* and all of the people are his slaves and servants only.

Islam came to establish peace and security as this is known from its root letters *Silm*, but there are those who spread mischief and disorder and become a threat to peace, and without controlling them there cannot be peace. This control sometimes needs fighting and the very first battle must be a Message to the miscreants and a lesson for them. So, when the *Prophet* established the first state in *Medina* based on *Qur'an* and *Sunnah*, and the people of *Makkah* used to instigate people against him in the surrounding areas, the *Prophet* used to send expeditions towards the people in places where he was informed of any uprising. But when the people of *Makkah* arranged a well-equipped army of more than 1000 people to destroy his base once for all, the *Prophet* faced them at *Badr* having only 313 people with fewer weapons. Since they were fighting for a noble cause, they fought wholeheartedly and *Allah* helped them defeat their enemy, killed 70 of them and captured another 70, and the *Prophet* then asked his two close associates *Abu Bakr* and *Umar* what should be done with these people? *Umar* said that they are criminals who turned us out of our homes, and for turning us out of our homes, killing us, instigating others against us and now attacking us, they should be killed. *Abu Bakr* said they should be released and, ultimately, they were released.

In verse 8:67-68 Allah says,

> *"This is not for a prophet to have captives until he shed blood in the land. You desire the commodities of this world while Allah wants (for you) the Hereafter. And Allah is All-Mighty, All-Wise. If there would not have been*

a decree already from Allah, you would have been touched by a grave punishment for what you have taken."

This is because from those who had resources, the *Prophet* took some ransom of them, so *Allah* said why you people were capturing them in the battlefield. You should have killed them when the fight was going on to pass a Message to them, so they may not try to attack you in the future. While they receive a Message. Yes, it is a part of the game to have captives, but now when you have captured them and released them for ransom, then this is lawful as a prior decree of *Allah* is there and in our research, this is about verse 47:4 which states,

"When you counter (in the battle) those who disbelieve then strike their necks until you have shed blood, then tie them firmly (capture them) and then either set them free for favor or for ransom until the war lays down its burden."

So, this was a rule, but it says that after that you shed blood they are in fear, then capture them, but now when you have done it then that is permissible.

IS IT A MUST TO HAVE CAPTIVES IN WAR?

In the battle of *Khaybar* the *Prophet* did not take the people of *Ghitfan* tribe as captives, but he let them pay *Jizyah* and enjoy their freedom. He did the same to the Jews in *Khaybar*.

Umar did so to the people of Iraq. He neither made them prisoners of war, nor did he take their belongings. So, it is not a must to make prisoners in war.

WHAT SHOULD BE DONE TO THE PRISONERS?

To make prisoners in war is also a type of protection that their life is saved.

In verse 9:6 *Allah* says,

> "And if someone from the polytheists asked for shelter (protection), so give him protection until he hears the words of Allah, then take him to the place of his safety."

The verse gave an implicit instruction that he may be put in such a place where he hears the talk about religion. Maybe he will get convinced and accept the *Deen* of *Islam* and become a *Muslim*, which is best for him in the eyes of *Allah*.

The *Prophet* said that even the lowest (common man) gives a binding shelter, meaning even if a common soldier gave it or promised it to someone then it must be honored and not to cause a breach of trust. *Imam*

Tirmizi narrated a *Hadith*. *Prophet* said that even if a woman sheltered one, it would be binding.

Abu Hurairah relates that the *Prophet* said,

> *"Whoever gave shelter to someone and then he killed him he would be given a flag (sign) of cheating on the Day of Judgment (Sharhus Sunnah)."*

It means he would be introduced to people as a traitor and cheater.

> *Imam Ahmad narrated in his Musnad that when Prophet married Jawairiyah, the daughter of the king of Banu Mustalaq from its captives, then Sahabah set free all the captives who were 100 or so, that they became the relatives of our Prophet. When Prophet was staying at Hudaibiyah as the people of Makkah stopped him from entering the House of Allah, so one day at Fajr time, some 80-people tried to attack their camp, but they all were captured by Sahabahs and brought to the Holy Prophet But he set them free (Muslim, Ahmad, Abu Dawud, Nisa'i, Tirmizi).*

> *Ahmad, Bukhari and Abu Dawud have narrated that in Hunain almost six thousand people were captured as prisoners of war. But when a delegation of Hawazin tribe approached the Prophet to set them free and, as they had been distributed to people, he addressed Sahabah that I have released the captives given to Banu Hashim i.e., the tribe of Prophet, so those who want to free them for free should do it, otherwise, set them free and I will compensate you in the near future. Same practice is known from Abu Bakr and Umar, the two successors of the Holy*

> *Prophet. In the case of captives of Badr the Prophet said, if Mut'im Ibni Adi was alive and would have asked me for these people I would have released them to him (Bukhari, Ahmad, Abu Dawud).*

And this was because when the *Prophet* was driven out of *Taif* and again he was going to *Makkah* he asked the help of this man and he helped him to enter *Makkah*, even when this man was not a *Muslim*.

When *Prophet* migrated to *Medina* the people of *Makkah* tried a few times to assassinate him, and in this regard the chief of *Tehama* (a vast area) was captured in *Medina* and brought to the *Prophet*. He admitted that he was there to kill *Muhammad*. The *Prophet* ordered him to be tied up with a pillar in the *Masjid* and ordered *Ali* to arrange for him some good food as he cannot eat our food. When the *Prophet* passed by him the *Prophet* asked him,

"What is your news?"

He said that if you kill you kill a man having blood (meaning his blood will not go away like this) and if you show kindness you showed it to a grateful one and if you need wealth, then ask how much. This was repeated for three days. Then *Prophet* released him. He went out to a garden, took a shower, came back, and took *Shahadah* and became *Muslim*. He said, your face to me was the most hated face on earth. But now that is the most beloved face to me.

Then, as the people of *Makkah* used to pass through his territory for their trade trips, he started taking everything of them. They cried to the *Prophet* that *Thumamah Ibni Athal* does not allow us to bring even the grain and our children are dying of hunger. The *Prophet* ordered him not to do this and let them have their necessities.

Now, the common rule is not to kill prisoners of war, except under some exceptional situations. These situations are either they are wanted in certain other cases, which required execution or they committed war crimes. That's why some scholars are of the view that the verses in *Surat Ul Anfal* abrogated the verse of *Surah Muhammad*.

The verse 47:42 of *Surah Muhammad* says,

> *"So, when you counter (in the battle) those who disbelieved then smite (their) necks until you spill (their) blood, then tie them up firmly and then after that either free them for favor or ransom (them)."*

And the verses 8:67-69 of *Surat Ul Anfal* state,

> *"This is not for a prophet to have captives until he spills blood in the land. You want the wealth of this world while Allah wants the Hereafter (for you) and Allah is All-Mighty, All-Wise. If there would not have been a decree already given by Allah, then for sure, a grievous torment from Allah would have afflicted you. So, eat what you have fetched as Booty and fear Allah. Verily, Allah is Oft-Forgiving, Most Merciful."*

Considering both situations, it is clear that the verses of *Anfal* confirm the concept stated in *Surah Muhammad* as ransom is mentioned in *Surah Muhammad* and *Allah* referred to that rule in the verse of *Surat Ul Anfal* that this ransom is already allowed, otherwise, you would have faced a torment even though this is not the first choice in the battlefield to capture people, but to fight first and later when some people get captured there will be either favor or ransom.

Also, when *Allah* blamed them for this ransom, they thought that whatever had been taken from them would be unlawful to eat, so in verse 69 *Allah* said,

> "So eat of what you have fetched as booty as lawful, pure."

This also affirmed that the concept stated in *Surah Muhammad* is intact and when one concept, i.e., the ransom is affirmed, the other one that is setting them free for favor is also affirmed. Some scholars said that to set them free is not allowed and especially for favor. And if we say that the verse of *Surat Ul Anfal* has abrogated the verse of *Surah Muhammad*, there will be no concept of capturing. There will, however, be a battle, since the verse says,

> "This is not for a prophet to have captives."

Yes, after a blood shed. That is why the majority say that it depends on the situation and circumstances. So, to ransom them, that is the *Madhab* of *Jumhur* and same is the saying of *Imam Abu Hanifa* as *Imam Muhammad* said it in *Assiyarul Kabir*.

The favor mentioned in the verse of *Surah Muhammad* starts with kindness to them when they are captured. The *Prophet* said, *Istousu Bil Osara Khaira* Have my order of kindness regarding captives.

The brother of *Mus'ab Ibni Umar*, namely *Abu Aziz* was brought as a captive in Badr. The *Prophet* gave him to an *Ansar* family to keep him with them and take care of him. He says that the family used to eat dates only but arrange food and bread for him.

Suhail Ibni Amr who was an orator of the people of *Makkah*, a table talker having the ability to convince for or against in any situation, was sent to the *Prophet* at the time of *Hudaibiyah* was amongst the prisoners of *Badr*. Some *Sahabah* said to the *Prophet* to order his teeth be broken so that he may not speak against them again. But the *Prophet* said if I break his teeth then *Allah* will break my teeth.

Hajjaj Ibni Yusuf asked *Abdullah Ibni Umar* to kill a prisoner. He handed him over to him but he refused and referred to this verse of *Surah Muhammad*.

Now kindness is forever and the captives are to be set free for free. The *Prophet* set many captives free. The ransom for them could be either in the form of money or for some specific services that they will render for a specific time and then they will be released. Regarding the captives of *Badr*, those who were literate the *Prophet* ordered them to teach so many children of *Ansar* how to read and write and then they would get a release while sometimes they could be released in exchange of *Muslim* prisoners if there were any. This means that it depends on situations. The righteous successors in their times adopted the same practice.

In one of the missions *Salamah Ibnul Akwa* was with *Abu Bakr*. Among the prisoners he captured, one women was very pretty. The *Prophet* exchanged that woman for two *Muslim* prisoners. *Imam Ahmed, Muslim* and *Tirmizi* narrated from *Imran Ibni Hussain* that *Banu Thaqeef* once captured two *Muslims,* and *Muslims* also captured one man from their allies, *Banu Aqeel*. The *Prophet* exchanged him for two of his prisoners. From *Banu Quraizah's* rebellion when *Sad Ibni Musa*, whom they asked to be the judge, he ordered the killing of their fighters and to make their children slaves and to confiscate their properties, then one *Zabeer Ibni Bata* who had sheltered *Thabit Ibni Qais* in the battle of *Bu'aath*, the *Prophet* gave him to *Thabit* to reciprocate his goodness and the *Prophet* also forgave *Amir Ibni Sad* as he used to ask the Jews to not break the treaty as this is treason. *Abu Bakr* released *Ash'ath Ibni Qais* and *Umar* released *Huvmuzan* and the captives of *Manazir* and *Meisan*. To release prisoners is a known concept. Yes, *Imam Abu Hanifa* said to do so if the circumstances require. Sometimes for giving a Message to the enemies for their wrongdoings some jurists allowed them to kill some prisoners. But if we will consider those cases it seems that they were killed for some crimes or cheating like from the prisoners of *Badr*, *Nadr Ibnul Harith* and *Oqbah Ibni Abi Moeet* got it. They both used to hurt the *Prophet* mentally and physically. They had killed *Abu Halah*, so they were killed. *Abu Azzah,* a poet, used to insult *Muslims* with his derogatory poetry. He was captured in *Badr*. But as he cried to *Prophet* that he had only two daughters and nobody was there to take care of them, he promised that he will never do what he used to do. But he broke his promise and became more aggressive, so when he was captured in *Uhud* again, he started to play the same dirty game but the *Prophet* said, a *Muslim* should not be bitten twice from the same hole and ordered his killing.

In *Khaybar, Kinanah Ibni Abil Huqaiq* himself asked for a treaty that they would leave everything for their lives to be saved.

The *Prophet* said,

"And if you will cheat then you people will be killed,"

to which he agreed. He buried a lot of gold and wealth in an abandoned place but someone informed the *Prophet*. When it was discovered, he was ordered to be killed.

And as we have mentioned, 15 people were declared to be killed at the conquest of *Makkah* for different crimes that they had committed. But only four of them were ultimately killed and the others were pardoned.

The *Prophet* said,

> "Do not kill an injured one, nor follow the one who is running away, nor kill any captive and whosoever closed his door, then leave him (Futuhul Buldan)."

This was at the conquest of *Makkah*. The people of *Makkah* had done to the *Prophet* and *Muslims* what they had done, but the *Prophet* said,

> "You are free. I do not want to charge you for what you had done."

If a non-*Muslim* accepted *Islam* in the battle then he may not be made a captive, but if someone is captured and been given to a *Muslim* as a slave, then he is a slave, but a *Muslim*. Imam Muslim and *Tirmizi* narrated from *Imran Ibni Husain* that a man from *Banu Aqeel* was captured, so he said, *"I accept Islam"* The *Prophet* said, if you would have said it before you were captured you would have been free. *Umar* said, if a captive accepted *Islam* in the hands of *Muslims* he got saved, but he is a slave.

SLAVERY AND SLAVES

It is an important issue as to whether prisoners of war could be enslaved.

Before *Islam* there were two types of slavery:

I. They used to enslave people by force. This practice was going on everywhere such as the people from Africa were brought as slaves to the United States of America and the rest of the American continent. *Arabs* also were doing the same to strangers passing by, they caught them and enslaved them. *Zaid Ibi Haritha* was a slave of this type until the *Holy Prophet* set him free. In *Islam* this type of slavery was dropped from day one.

II. Prisoners of war were also enslaved. This was a universal practice and they used to live as slaves for their lifetime. Now this was such a practice that *Islam* could not drop it one sided as the enemies made *Muslims* slaves and if *Muslims* did not do it, it wouldn't work. So, *Islam* kept this basic concept and its title, but reformed it to such an extent that certain people were proud of being slaves of certain people because the *Prophet* said,

"Treat them like your own family member."

And as we have mentioned, a good majority of authorities in *Islam* for *Tafsir*, *Hadith* laws and Jurisprudence, were themselves slaves or their children.

The *Prophet* said,

> *"Feed them what you eat and dress them with the dress like yours and do not overburden them and when you assign them some duty then help them."*

This *Hadith* is narrated by *Abu Zar Al Ghifari*.

Someone asked the *Prophet* how many times one can overlook his slave.

The *Prophet* said,

> *"You should forgive them every day 70 times."*

The *Prophet* also said,

> *"Make your slave to sit with you on the same dining or at least you should put a few morsels of your food in his mouth."*

The reward that the *Prophet* used to mention for kindness that one shows to his slaves, so many *Sahabah* (companions of the *Prophet*) got slaves for the said purpose as some of them married slave girls to make them *Ummal Walad*, which means to have child from her so that she may get the respect and freedom right after the death of her master.

The *Prophet* said,

> *"Whosoever had a slave girl, he gave her a good training and best education, set her free and then he married her, he will have two rewards (for every good deed)."*

Imam Hussain married a slave-girl from *Persia* and got a great *Imam* from the lady who is known as *Imam Zainul Abideen*. Among *Tabi'een*, there are known and famous jurists who were the children of slaves like *Hasan Basri* whose father was a slave. *Imam Muhammad Ibni Sirin* was the son of a slave father and slave mother. *Nafi*, the student of *Ibni Umar* and the teacher of *Imam Abu Hanifa* and *Malik* was a slave himself. The mothers of *Salim Ibni Abdullah* and *Qasim Ibni Muhammad Ibni Abi Bakr* were slaves. The grandfather of *Imam Abu Hanifa* was a slave of *Bani Taimullah, Abdullah Ibnul Mubarak*, the *Ameerul Momineen* in *Hadith*, was the son of a slave named *Mubarak*.

Bilal Ibni Abi Rabah, the famous *Sahabi*, was a slave. He called *Azan* at *Medina* in the times of *Prophet* and whom *Prophet* ordered at the time of the conquest of *Makkah* to go to the roof top of the Holy *Ka'ba* to call *Azan*. *Umar Ibnul Khattab* used to say, he is our master. *Salman Al Farsi* was an *Iranian* slave.

Prophet said,

"he is from my family."

This, he said, when he advised a trench to be dug to the open side of *Medina* at the battle of confederates and thus *Medina* was protected. So, *Ansar* said, he is from us and *Muhajireen* said, he is from us. Then the *Prophet* said, he is from my family.

When *Umar* was hit by *Abu Lulu* and suffering from injuries, he said that if *Salim*, the liberated slave of *Abu Huzaifah*, would have been alive I would have appointed him as *Khalifa* and if *Allah* would have asked me, why I would have said, because your *Prophet* said, Allah loves this man. *Ummi Aiman* was the slave of the father of the *Prophet* whom he inherited. She was the nursing lady for the *Prophet*.

Once the *Prophet* said,

> "Who wants to marry a lady from Paradise he should marry Ummi Aiman,"

so, *Zaid Ibni Haritha* married her and she had his son *Osamah Ibni Zaid* from her who was the beloved of the *Prophet*, like *Hassan* and *Hussain*.

Abu Masud Al Ansari said,

> "Once I raised my hand on my slave, suddenly I heard someone saying Allah has more power on you than you have on your slave. I saw this was the Prophet of Allah. So, I said, then he is free."

The *Prophet* said that if you would not have done that then the fire would have touched you.

Imam Bukhari and *Muslim* related a *Hadith* that the Prophet said,

> "Whosoever set a slave free Allah will let him be free from fire for every organ of the slave an organ of this master, even his private part for his private part."

Imam Bayhaqi narrated that a *Bedouin* asked the *Holy Prophet*,

> "Tell me about an action by which I can go to Paradise."

The *Prophet* said,

"Emancipate a slave."

So, *Islam* has mentioned a few ways to set slaves free:

EMANCIPATION OF SLAVES

Islam has mentioned a few ways to set slaves free:

1. To emancipate a slave to please *Allah*.

2. To make him *Mudabbar*, which means to say to him,

    "you are free after my death."

This word is binding. Neither the master who said it, nor the slave, can withdraw or reject it. Now that slave could not be sold, nor gifted, nor inherited. Yes, the only thing the master can do is to let him free in his lifetime. Otherwise he will get free after the death of his master anyway.

3. To have his own slave-girl like one has his wife means to have sexual relationship with her and when she will deliver a child, she becomes *Ummul Walad*.

Not only does she get respect being the mother of the child of her mast, but automatically she becomes like a *Mudabbar* that she will have freedom right after the death of her master.

4. To make him *Mukatab Allah* says in verse 24:33,

> *"And those who seek "Kitabat" (contract of becoming free when they will pay the appointed amount) from among whom your hands possess (own), male or female) then do "Kitabat" with them if you think of goodness in them, and give them from the wealth of Allah which he has given you."*

In this verse,

- *"If you think (feel) goodness in them"* means that they can earn and they can give what is agreed upon,

- *"And give them from the wealth of Allah"* means *Zakat* and charity i.e., help them with that, so that they may pay the amount and be freed. They are of one of the eight categories to whom the *Zakat* may be given as that is stated in verse 9:60.

5. *Islam* is that much eager then when it put *Kafarat* (atonement/expiation) for certain things like -

   a. mistaken and accidental killing of someone,

   b. *Zihar*, if someone said to his wife, *"To me you are like the back of my mother,"*

   c. breaking one's oath, or

   d. breaking his fasting during *Ramadan* without any just reason.

In all these cases he is bound to pay *Kaffarah* to take off the burden of his conscience and to have the sin forgiven. So, one way of that *Kaffarah* is to set a slave free.

6. If a slave is owned by two people and one of them sets his portion free, now if this one is rich then he must pay the other partner his portion to make the slave free and if he is not rich, the slave has become the like of *Mukatab* in the remaining portion, so he may be given a free hand to earn and to pay that remaining half to be free, so that he may be helped with *Zakat* and other charities as well. This is the saying of *Malik, Shafi', Ahmad, Abu Yusuf* and *Muhammad*.

NOTE: (a) The *Kitabat* contract is binding from the master side, so he cannot take it back. But if the slave wants to dissolve it he has this right. (b) If the master said to his slave that you are free or I made you *Mudabbar* and then says that he was not serious but joking, he is bound by his words.

Slavery was not introduced by *Islam*, but considered by Islam as it was going on and could not be dropped one-sided. So, when the whole world agreed that there should not be any slavery, then *Islam* said the same thing.

AL WALA WAL BARA

(ASSOCIATION AND DISASSOCIATION)

The whole world is created by *Allah* and originated from one and the same source. Its origin is one and the same. All living creatures came from black, sticky, smelly mud. Mankind came from the same mud as well, as in verse 15:26 *Allah* says,

> *"And indeed, We created man out of clay from an altered black, smelly mud."*

Also, in verse 23:12 He says,

> *"And indeed, We created man from the extract (nucleus) of clay."*

And in verse 32:7-8 He says,

> *"And He started the creation of man from clay and then He made his posterity out of the extract (nucleus) of a disdained liquid."*

So, every human has the same origin and the same procedure, which means original similarity and equality as everyone is from the same couple, *Adam* and *Eve*, or everyone is from one father and one mother, as in verse 4:1 *Allah* says,

> *"O mankind! Fear your Lord Who created you from one soul (Adam) and created from him his mate (Eve) and dispersed from both of them many men and women."*

In verse 49:13 *Allah* says,

> *"O mankind! Indeed, We created you from one man and one woman."*

Now, this one man and one woman are *Adam* and *Eve*, or the real father and real mother of everyone that everyone is born of one father and one mother, which again means the original equality. While after that are tribes. As they are coming down they are divided into tribes, caste, clans, etc. Because of human nearness and immediate affiliation, they are much more influenced than they think by their nearest ancestors, predecessors and off-springs first, and then extending that to others. As we live in different countries, so our affiliation to the country in which we live is closer, even dearer, to us than other countries and this is natural.

And as we see that there are certain affiliations like the one to our family, another to our tribe and nation, another to our country, another to our faith or another to our ethnic group or political party, this affiliation differs from people to people. Some people have a stronger affiliation to their clan than their religion, others have stronger affiliation to their country than their faith, and still some others have a stronger affiliation to their faith than to anything else. And faith is even stronger than anything else in majority of the people, whatever their faith may be and that's why all civilized laws say that religious sentiments of no one may be harmed because people tolerate it very rarely.

In verse 6:108 *Allah* says,

> *"And do not insult (abuse/vilify) those who invoke (worship) others besides Allah, lest they insult Allah in enmity ignorantly. Thus, we have made fair seeming to every group their actions. Then to your Lord is their return, so that he will inform them about what they used to do."*

But all that we said is that affiliations and connections between people differ from people to people and things to things and we are living in such a world. We have the intellect, so we may use it to handle things and situations to live in peace and harmony. We may not disconnect from people as a whole as that is against the very nature and especially for the *Ummah* of *Prophet Muhammad* who are messengers of the Messenger of *Allah* and they are bound to convey His Message to others in common practices of theirs more than words This is possible only if they have connections with others.

Now-a-days, *Muslims* either abuse this, misuse it, or do not use it at all and as *Islam* is the religion of *Allah* the religion of messengers and the religion of humans or for humans in general a religion of peace and justice and a balanced religion, which has given basic rules for every situation, so this is now the duty of *Muslims* to find out as to how to apply these rules, which one is to be applied and where?

Therefore, *Wala* and *Bara* are known to be a very important topic. So, we will quote here verses regarding this topic and then analyze them to determine the relevant limits and conditions:

1. Verses 3:28-29 say,

> *"Let not believers take disbelievers as allies against the believers and whoever does that then he has nothing from Allah (in his sight), but if you take a precaution from them and Allah warns you of Himself and to Allah is your return. Say, if you conceal what is in your chests (hearts) or reveal it, Allah knows it and He knows whatsoever is there in the heavens and on earth and Allah is competent over all things."*

ANALYSIS:

Any friendship with disbelievers that goes against believers (meaning from their religion point of view) is prohibited. Yes, as a precaution or in seeking protection from them that is allowed as that is a need, but this should not be an excuse to say, *"Oh! We did it because of that"* as *Allah* has warned believers of Himself in the same verse and in the following, that He knows everything. So, a lame excuse is not a good excuse. He said that your final return is to Him and He can do anything, which means that He can punish you in this world along with their protection that you sought and in the Hereafter, He will hold you accountable.

2. Verses 3:118-119 say,

> *"O you who believed! Do not take as "Bitanah" (secrecy advisors) other than your own (or against your own people) as they will not spare you the ruin. They wish your fall in hardships. Hatred is already obvious from their mouths (words) and what their chests conceal it is even bigger (than these words). We have certainly made it clear to you the signs, if you will use sense. O you are*

those who love them while they do not love you. You believe in all the scriptures (but they do not believe so). And when they meet you they say, we believe but when they are alone they bit their fingertips at you in rage. Say, die in your rage (or along with your rage or due to your rage). Verily, Allah is All-Knowing of what is in the breasts."

ANALYSIS:

Bitanah means hidden or secret, which here means that disbelievers may not be your secrecy advisors as they will never keep your secrets and if that is regarding the affairs of your state, that will cause you a big loss and ruin. The wording *Min Doon* means except and against. In most of such verses it means against—i.e., against the believer, which causes a problem in *Deen*, then that type of relation with disbelievers is forbidden. But here it can mean except yourselves meaning the keepers of the secret of an *Islamic* state must be from believers as they have loyalty to the state through its ideology and they know what is good for the *Deen* and state and what is not good. This is the case for every state that the one who does not believe in the very ideology of the state which is the foundation of their system, will never put him in a sensitive position. For example, someone who is not a citizen by birth cannot contest the election to be the head of the state or the government in certain countries even though he is a naturalized citizen, or someone who has a foreigner spouse, as his or her mate cannot oversee the foreign affairs of the state or other sensitive posts so that the secrets may not be disclosed to a foreigner. *Islam*, as a system, is to be considered as ideology of the state or in a broader sense a state itself, so this disbeliever is to be considered as a stranger to it, especially if he does not hail from the same *Islamic* state.

In verse 9:16 *Allah* says the same.

Verse 7:16 says,

> "Do you think you will be left be left alone and Allah would not have separated those who strived hard from among you and have not taken other than Allah and His Messenger and believers anyone as "Waleejah."

This *Waleejah* and *Bitanah* have the same meanings as intimate or secrecy keeper – that such people are the tested ones.

3. Verses 4:138-140 say,

> "Give tidings to hypocrites that for them there is a painful torment. Those who take disbelievers as friends/protectors against believers, do they seek with them the honor, so the honor belongs to Allah entirely while He has sent down to you in the Book that when you hear the verses of Allah being rejected and ridiculed (by them) then do not sit with them until they enter into another talk. Verily, at that time you will be the like of them. Indeed, Allah will gather together hypocrites and disbelievers in Hell."

ANALYSIS:

These verses make it clear that friendship with disbelievers that goes against *Islam* and *Islamic* faith is either done by hypocrites or such people become hypocrites by doing so. Also, *Allah* mentions that they do it seeking for some honor, but honor can be given by *Allah* alone. He also forbade one to sit in a place where people mock the *Deen* and the concepts of the *Deen* of *Islam*. This is not only about disbelievers, but sometime some so-called *Muslims* do the same. Then sitting with them quietly is hypocrisy. So, one who is a disbeliever and he does that, but a *Muslim* who can make a way out, if he cannot stop him but he did not leave, then he is committing hypocrisy and then *Allah* warns that such hypocrites would be thrown in the Fire together with those disbelievers. Yes, if some *Muslim* got stuck there in such a way that he can neither make his way out, nor can he stop them from that mockery but in his heart, he thinks them and their doing bad, then that can be an excuse. Then after these verses *Allah* expressed His prohibition and in verse 4:144 He says,

> *"O you who believed! Do not take disbelievers as your "Auliya" helpers, protectors or friends) against believers. Do you wish to give Allah against yourselves a clear proof?"*

4. Verses 5:51-53 say,

> *"O you who believed! Do not take the Jews and Christians as "Auliya" (friends, protectors). They are friends of each other and whosoever will take them as "Auliya" (helpers, protectors) then he is one of them. Indeed, Allah does not guide the wrongdoing people. Then you will see those in whose hearts there is an ailment (of cowardice, weakness and hypocrisy) rushing towards them to say, we fear that some misfortune will strike us. But it may be that Allah will bring a conquest or something else from his side and they will be ashamed of what they did. And those who believed they will say (regarding these cowards), "Are these the people who swore by Allah their strongest oath that they are for sure with you. Their actions have become worthless and they have become losers."*

ANALYSIS:

Here, *Allah* specifically mentions the Jews and Christians as they were friends at that time, so we must take into consideration that condition *Min Doon* means friendship or alliance that goes against *Islam* and *Muslims* regarding their *Deen* and faith, because the case of Muslims with Jews and Christians is a little bit different than that of with other non-*Muslims* or disbelievers because it is permissible for *Muslims* to eat the meat they slaughter in the name of *Allah* or marry a Jew or Christian woman as *Allah* said in verse 5:5,

> *"And the food (meat) of those who were given a Scripture is lawful for you and your food is lawful for them and also the chaste women from among believers and the chaste women from among those who were given the Scripture before you (are lawful for you)."*

In verse 29:46 *Allah* says,

> *"And do not argue with the People of Book but in a way which is best, except those who commit injustice from among them and say, we believed in that which has been sent down to us and which is sent down to you, and our God and your God is one and we submit to Him."*

And in verses 5:55-58 *Allah* explains further and says,

> *"Indeed, your "Wali" (helper, protector) is Allah, His Messenger and those who believed, perform the prayer, give "Zakat" and they bow down (to Allah) and whosoever will befriend Allah, His Messenger and those who believed, then for sure, the party of Allah are the prominent (overcoming). O you who believed! Do not take those who use your "Deen" for ridicule and amusement from among those who were given the Book before you,*

and disbelievers (as well) as "Auliya" (helpers, friends) and fear Allah if you are but believers. And when you call for prayers they take it in ridicule and amusement. That is because they are a people who do not use sense (reason)."

ANALYSIS:

Here, there is the same issue. But *Allah* mentions a specific thing that when some people are ridiculing your faith and rituals, how can you befriend them and go along with? If you do that, it is going against your own belief if you stay quiet, and if not then it will take you towards a fight, so the best way is to stay away of such like insensible people. This is the reason why *Allah* said in the end that ridiculing the *Deen* of others or their rituals is their non-sense, as this harms the religious sentiments and that is against every civilized law.

Then *Allah* mentioned this disassociation of a symbol of the true believers as in verse 58:22 He said,

> *"You will not find a people who believe in Allah and the Last Day having affection for those who oppose Allah and His Messenger even if they are their fathers or their sons or their brothers and their kindred. Those He has put in their hearts faith and supported them with the spirit from Him and He will admit them to gardens under which there are rivers flowing abiding therein forever. Allah is pleased with them and they are pleased with Him. They are the party of Allah. Behold! The party of Allah is the successful one."*

So, now this is clear that true believers do not disconnect themselves for no reason from people, and when a solid reason is there they disconnect themselves even from their kith and kin because *Allah* has warned those who befriend the enemies of *Allah* against the *Deen* of *Allah* as in verses 9:23-24 He said,

> *"O you who believed! Do not take your fathers or your brothers as "Auliya" (friends or allies) if they prefer disbelief over belief and whosoever does so among you then they are wrongdoers. Say (O Muhammad), if your fathers, your sons, your brothers, your mates, your relatives (or friends), the wealth which you have obtained, the businesses you fear its decline, the houses you like, are more beloved to you, from Allah, His Messenger and from "Jihad" in His cause then wait until Allah will execute His command and Allah does not guide defiantly disobedient people."*

Again, the condition *Min Doon* is meant to mean that friendship which goes against the *Deen* as it is said in the end

> *"if these are more beloved to you then Allah, His Messenger and Jihad in His cause."*

5. Verses 60:1-2 say,

> *"O you who believed! Do not take My enemy and your enemy as "Auliya" (friends, protectors) extending to them affection while they have disbelieved in what came to you of the Truth ("Deen") having driven out the Prophet and you (as well) because you believe in Allah, your Lord, if you have come out for "Jihad" in My path and to seek My pleasure. You confide in them affection*

while I know well what you have concealed and what you have revealed. And whoever does it among you, then for sure, he has lost the sound path. If they get a dominance over you they shall be your enemies and they shall extend against you their hands and their tongues and they will wish you to disbelieve."

ANALYSIS:

In these verses there are a few points:

i. The *Muslims* may consider the enemies of *Allah* their enemies as there is no room for friendship with the enemies of *Allah*, especially when they have not only rejected the Truth, but also turned you and the *Prophet* out from your homes and homeland.

ii. Furthermore, when you are in *Jihad* in situations certain rules are changed and certain things are forbidden which were, otherwise, allowable under normal circumstances.

iii. These things that we discussed in detail have been made clear in verses 60:8-9 to say,

"Allah does not forbid you from those who did not fight against you on account of the "Deen", nor expelled you from your homes, to be kind to them and deal with them justly. Indeed, Allah loves the just people. Allah only forbids you from those who fight against you on account of the "Deen" and turned you out of your homes and aided in your expulsion, to have friendship with them. And whoever befriends them then they are wrongdoers."

ANALYSIS:

Verse 8 makes it clear that kindness should be shown to those disbelievers who did not wrong you because of your *Deen*. This can be a way to convince them to practically think about you and your *Deen* in a positive light.

The mother of *Asmah Bint Abi Bakr* came to *Medina* to meet her daughter. Her name was *Qateelah Bint Abdul Uzza*. She had brought some gifts too, but *Asma* did not let her enter her house as she was not *Muslim*. So, *Aisha* asked the *Prophet*. He recited verse 8, then *Asma* let her enter her house and gave her the respect of a mother *(Ahmad, Hakim)*.

Also, in verses 31:14-15 *Allah* says,

> *"And We have enjoined man (to do good) for his parents. His mother carried him in weakness after weakness and his weaning is in two years, to pay thanks to Me and to your parents. To Me is the return and if they both endeavor to make you associate with Me that of which you have no knowledge then do not obey them, but accompany them in this world in a good way, and follow the way of one who inclined to Me."*

ANALYSIS:

Here also, *Allah* ordered kindness to parents, even if they ask their children to make partners with *Allah*. It means that they may not be obeyed for things going against the *Deen*, but still the children must respect them.

NOTE: Here it is important to differentiate between person-to-person relation and state-to-state relation.

Person means:

a) *Muslim* living in an *Islamic* state,

b) *Muslim* living in a non-*Muslim* state,

c) Non-*Muslim* living in a *Muslim* state,

d) Non-*Muslim* living in a non-*Muslim* state.

So, all of them are the citizens of their own countries, so they live therein as law abiding citizens and whatever promises they have made to the state they must be honest to that as the *Prophet* said,

> "*Muslims must stop with their conditions (promises), meaning to fulfill these.*"

The citizens have equal rights.

There are exceptions in certain areas as we mentioned some before, for example, a naturalized citizen cannot contest for presidency or a key post or posts related to state secrecy, and it is considered as being for security of the state and not discrimination. Each state has its own secrecies, so it can place certain conditions on certain groups. For example, regarding individual dealings, everyone is a citizen having equal rights as we discussed in detail. The case is that of state-to-state relation, so in the international community the state is a legal person having its own duties and responsibilities like a natural person and as a natural person has his own status and he is looking out for his own good and interests, same is the case of states. But this is subject to doing no harm to others in the cases of both individuals and states, because there is no boundless freedom like the one who was playing with his stick swinging it through his fingers that hit the nose of one besides him and he showed his reaction to him, who then said,

> *"I am a free man and this is my freedom."*

The other man said,

> *"Gentleman! Your freedom ends where my nose begins,"*

meaning freedom has limits and that is why it is said that freedom is fire. If it is not contained, it will burn you as well.

Even if states are not for fight, still it happens.

The *Prophet* said,

> *"Do not wish facing your enemies and ask Allah peace and security. But if you faced them then be stable."*

While nobody knows what will happen in the future, if the relationship of *Muslim* and non-*Muslim* states are sound and solid, but what will be the position of *Muslim* state as a matter of policy?

Imams Malik, *Shafi'* and *Ahmad* said that the basis of relationship should be peace, while *Imam Abu Hanifa* said, this relationship is basically and should be that of caution, which means that *Islamic* state may be prepared if something happens unexpectedly from the other side. It doesn't mean that it should start a war, but it means that if the other side cheated and broke their treaty then there should not be any excuse for *Islamic* state that they trusted them, that's why they were not ready. In such a case it will lose its sovereignty.

In verses 8:60-62 *Allah* says,

> *"And prepare against them whatever you are able of power and steed by which you may frighten the enemy of Allah and your enemy and others besides them whom you*

> *do not know (but) Allah knows them and whatever you spend in the path of Allah (it) will be fully repaid to you and you will not be wronged. And if they are inclined to peace then incline you to it (also) and put your trust in Allah. Verily, He is All-Hearer, All-Knower, and if they intend to deceive you then sufficient for you is Allah. He is the One Who helped you with His help and by the believers."*

These verses make it clear that *Muslims* must be ready and have weapons, but that is a deterrent and a security for your state, and while threat mostly comes from the outside, it can be from the inside as well like the uprising by miscreants, and if they come to know that the state does not have enough defense, then this will encourage them to proceed further and that is what is meant by

> *"and others whom you do not know but Allah knows them."*

So, this weapon is to control the situation so that nothing may happen. Still *Allah* said that even if they started a war and you retaliated, but if they incline to peace then you may inline to it as well. Yes, you may have reservations that they will try to cheat. But *Allah* said, you may rely on *Allah*, because if there is an ongoing mistrust then there will be no peace forever.

In the *Islamic* laws on international relations it is clearly mentioned that a state cannot live in isolation as a state represents a population made of humans and humans are social by nature. The same is true for an *Islamic* state that it will have relations with other states but they must have it because for non-*Muslims* that is a social, political and an economical need and requirement. But for *Muslims* that is religious as well because there is no *Prophet* after *Prophet Muhammad*, and they are representing him in his Message and humans need to hear it, so they must be in touch and have good relations with others to convey his Message to them. It is their duty to be as Just and kind towards them that they may are fully convinced to accept this Message.

The interstate relations must be based upon honesty, truthfulness, justice, equity, and equality, especially from the *Muslim's* side as these are their religious commandments and orders.

Yes, now-a-days the world is a place where *Jihad* is inevitable according to is condition and pre-requisites there are those who are bound to declare it. If they do not do that it may be because of their own reasons or sometime where there is no room to launch *Jihad*, then there the irrelevant people start it. Both ways bring disorder, even turmoil and common people fall prey to it. In other words, *Jihad* is either not used or misused or abused. So, no *Jihad* brings a lot of disorder in the same way the misuse or abuse of it is counter-productive.

The order of *Allah* in verse 9:124 says,

> "*Fight those adjacent to you of the disbelievers and let them find in your toughness*"

gives us a few pointers:

i. Do it when it becomes incumbent on you according to the circumstances.

ii. The close-by people may fight, which means from far they may not plunge in as sometimes it causes more difficulties and basically that is the duty of the nearby *Muslims*.

Now, in the end we will request everyone regardless of their religious connection to read this Book with a clear mind and heart, not with a pre-conditioned mind set. We are sure the propaganda that is going on against *Islam* is wrong. Yes, some *Muslims* could be wrong in what they are doing by using the name of *Islam* or *Islamic* terms. But people should not be the criterion for a religion, rather the religion should be the criterion. Otherwise, this wrong approach will produce only wrongs. So, let's learn once again the lesson of co-existence that

> *"Live and let others live"*

or

> *"accept yourself and accept others as well"*

because variety is the beauty of this world and as *Allah* says,

> *"We have made that which is on earth an adornment for it"*

MAY ALLAH GUIDE US TOWARDS THE REALITY AND TRUTH.

AMEEN

BOOKS BY QAZI FAZL ULLAH

Qazi Fazl Ullah has written other books. Below is a short list with summaries.

FIQH KEE TAREEKH WA IRTIQA (URDU)

Islam is *Deen* (religion) and is a complete code of life. Its laws are of two types, textual and deduced, but how the text is interpreted and how laws are deduced therefrom is called *"Jurisprudence"* and the laws are called *Fiqh,* and how this *Fiqh* got developed and compiled. This book gives the details about its stages of development.

MOHAMMADUR RASOOLULLAH (URDU)

The biography of the *Prophet Muhammad* was preserved from day one by his blessed companions. Then scholars and historians have written books in this regard in different times, both concise and detailed. This book on the biography of *Prophet Muhammad* is an excellent balance of concise and detailed, as a concise a book sometimes misses things and people do not have time to read and understand too detailed a book. Another important feature of this book is that almost with every important part of the *Prophet's* biography, the relevant part of the *Holy Quran* has been quoted, which illustrates that the *Prophet's* life was the practical shape of the *Holy Book*.

SARMAYA DARANA NIZAM ISHTIRAKIYAT AUR ISLAM (URDU)

Humans, throughout their history, have thought ahead and planned their economics and economical needs. They created systems for these purposes. The three systems most widely practiced in history are capitalism, communism, and *Islam*. This book is a comparative study of these 3 economical systems and it proves that the *Islamic* system bestowed upon us by the Creator is the best one with regard to justice and no room for exploitation.

DAWAT O JIHAD (URDU)

The basic duty of every *Prophet* and his followers was and is to call the people towards *Allah* in a peaceful, attractive, and convincing way, and wherever and whenever they encountered resistance and hindrances in this regard, they must remove these hindrances. At times, this leads to fights, as when the conspiracy is big and the opponents try to take away their fundamental rights, so they have the right to defend it but how, when, and where? In this book, it is mentioned that *Islam* teaches us to convey, convince, and convert, but not to coerce. This book is an answer to anti-*Islamic* propaganda, especially about the concept of *Jihad* in *Islam*.

ISLAM AUR SIYASAT (URDU)

Islam and Politics—as it is known from the title that this book discusses *Islamic* political system, because *Islam* is *Deen*, meaning a complete code of life and not a set of a few rituals. It has its own system for state and government. So, wherever *Muslims* are in power, if they will implement this system, they meet the needs of everyone, regardless of color, caste, or religion. *Islam* covers the details, such as how to elect a government, and how to run the state to provide peace and justice to all.

RIYASATI ISLAMI KA TASWWAR (URDU)

The title means the concept of an *Islamic* state, and *"concept"* means its conduct. In this book, it is mentioned how and why a state and government is needed, and how that state and government may be and should be run. The Creator *Allah* the Almighty knows all our needs, necessities, qualities and shortcomings, so the system he has given is the only system that can ensure people's security and safety and can provide them peace and justice, making the state a welfare state.

USOOLUT - TAFSEER (ARABIC)

Every branch of science has its own rules, principles and methodologies, which provide guidelines for explaining it and how to interpret it, so this methodology is a circle or limits one may keep himself confines to so he will not get lost or go astray.

This book covers the explanation of the *Holy Quran*, the last and final book of *Allah*. The book of *Allah* is the basic source of *Islam* and *Islamic* law, so its explanation requires certain rules to be followed in its explanation, so one may not be unbridled and without restraint, otherwise he will put his faith in danger.

DIRAYATUR RIWAYAH (ARABIC)

Hadith (sayings, actions and sanctions) of *Prophet Muhammad* is the second fundamental source of *Islam* and *Islamic* laws and also it is the interpretation of the *Holy Quran*. The companions of the *Prophet Muhammad* have preserved them in their memories and in their scriptures and the second and third generation took it from them and preserved them as well. Later on, when there was a fear of perversion, then these *Ahadith* were compiled officially and later on, the authentic scholars gathered them together in various books. Furthermore, critics compiled a biography of all these narrators and put certain rules about how a *Hadith* could be accepted. This book includes all these details.

HUJJIYATI HADITH (URDU)

This book is regarding the authenticity of *Hadith* of the *Prophet*, as there is a baseless propaganda that *Hadith* were not written in the time of the *Prophet*, but later on, making them unreliable. This is wrong, as *Sahaba* used to write *Ahadith* and sometimes the *Prophet* himself used to order them to write. But they trusted their memory more than writing. Official compilation took place later on, when *Muslim* rulers became aware of the weakness of people's memories and the loss of those individuals writing. This book provides all these details and makes it clear that *Hadith* is *Wahi* (Revelation) and source of *Islamic Shariah* (Law).

FUNDAMENTALISM, SECULARISM AUR ISLAM (URDU)

Propaganda is being spread either because of ignorance or with mala fide intention that *Islam* is fundamentalism.

Fundamentalism was a term used for Christianity when it blocked the ways of scientific research, invention and development, and some people wanted to adopt it as a basic guideline for states and government. So those who were with research and development branded that as fundamentalism. But *Islam* does not stop or block progress and research; rather, it encourages it and even orders scholars to go ahead and do research, as discussed in this book.

AL IJTIHADU WAT TAQLEED (URDU)

Humans are social and intellectual animals. They have all the same needs as animals, but they are distinct from them because of their intellect as they are looking for their ease, to do a little and get a lot. For this purpose, some intellectuals invent things and others follow them. Then as they are bound to obey the *Deen* of *Allah*, there are other intellectuals who deduce laws from its fundamental sources: the *Quran* and the *Sunnah*, and the less intellectuals follow them, as they should. This is the only intellectual and reasonable way. This book explains this issue and its importance.

MUSALMAN AURAT (URDU)

Allah created the world. He created humans and made them men and women. He gave different qualities to both genders for the smooth running of this life to depend upon each other, but as humans they are equal. Some women made history and they did memorable work that many men could not have done. This small book mentions some of the great work of some great women, particularly *Muslim* women, to make it clear that *Islam* deeply respects women and appreciates their contributions to society.

ASMATI RASOOL OR ZAWAJI AAISHA (URDU)

This world is a combination of opposites and some people have been given a great status. The *Messengers* of *Allah* are the chosen and beloved of *Allah*. He made them and built them up for himself and his work. They are the most respected and honored people, and they must be given respect, as any disgrace to them can harm the feelings and sentiments of their followers, which can cause trouble. In this book this issue is discussed, as well as a misconception about the *Prophet's* marriage to *Aaisha*; namely, that she was minor at that time. Academically and research fully, this book corrects this misconception.

AL FARA'ID FIL AQA'ID (ARABIC)

Aqeedah and *Aqa'id* means faith and beliefs, respectively, and they are the base of *Deen*. Certain beliefs are the contents of *Iman*. What is important for a *Muslim* to believe? These are detailed in this concise book. Some *Muslim* sects have misconstrued some of these beliefs, so the book mentions that as well and makes the right faith clear.

QAWA'IDUT - TAJWEED (ARABIC)

One of the basic duties of the *Prophet* was to teach his followers how to recite the holy book properly. His *Sahabah* learnt it from him and then this became a specific science in future generations. They not only taught their students the proper way of recitation, they also wrote books about it. This science is called *Tajweed*, which literally means to make good, but in this science, it means to recite good. This book prescribes the basic rules for *Tajweed* as proper pronunciation not only makes the words and sounds good but also helps in giving the proper meaning of the word.

AL QAWA'IDUL FIQHIYAH (ARABIC)

Islam is *Deen* and a complete system and code of life. For each and every aspect of life there are rules and laws in *Islam*. Some of these rules are in text of the *Quran* and the *Sunnah*, while some others are deduced therefrom. For deduction, the authentic jurists have laid down rules of deduction and the qualities required for themselves. Then, after deduction, they have found some commonalities in different laws in different chapters, so they laid down a common rule for that and these rules called *Al Qawa'idul - Fiqhiyah*, or legal maxims, which make the study of *Fiqh* easy and understandable. This book includes some known and famous legal maxims in all four schools of jurisprudence.

AL JIHAD FIL ISLAM (ARABIC)

Jihad is a very important issue in *Islam*; to defend life, property, honor and faith is not only a well-known right in each and every culture but also a duty in *Islam*, but how and when? This book is written on this subject. As this issue is quite controversial, this is a reasonable answer to these questions in the light of the *Quran* and *Sunnah*.

MAULANA UBAIDULLAH SINDHI (URDU)

Maulana Ubaidullah Sindhi, originally from a *Sikh* family, accepted *Islam* when he was a teenager. He studied *Deen* in the proper and traditional way, then joined the freedom movement. He went through a lot of difficulties, and lived in exile for 24 years. As a revolutionary leader, he is controversial and many people wrote against him as well as for him. This book describes his personality, struggle, and thoughts to know who he was and how he was.

ASMATI RASOOL AND KHATMI NUBUWWAT (URDU)

Asmati Rasool and *Khatmi Nubuwwat* are reasonable and logical. This book consists of two parts. The defense of the *Prophet* and that of him being the last and final *Prophet* of *Allah* is a reasonable and logical thing, as *Allah* sent *Messengers* in different times to different areas and different nations, and when they worked in their respected times in those areas, *Allah* sent the *Prophet Muhammad* to the entire world to combine their work and bring humanity together on the same theme, subject and faith that all those earlier *Messengers* were sent for. This book is a concise, detailed and logical interpretation of this finality.

SAYYIDAH AAISHA'S AGE AT MARRIAGE (ENGLISH)

Islam is a Natural *Deen* or *Deen* of Nature. This is a balanced *Deen* providing a comprehensive justice system, and the *Holy Prophet* is the perfect role model as a perfect human. His words, actions, and sanctions are the proper interpretation of the *Holy Quran* and the second fundamental source of laws in *Islam*. There is a commonly held belief, especially among critics of *Islam*, that the *Prophet* married *Aaisha* when she was only nine years of age. In this book, all the details about this issue is given that how this word *Tis'aa* (which means nine) happened there and what the real story is to counter the false accounts and correct the record.

JIHAD IN ISLAM : WHY, HOW, AND WHEN?

(ENGLISH)

Jihad as a word in *Arabic* means struggle or striving hard, especially for a noble cause, while as a term in *Islam*, it specifically means to fight in the path/cause of *Allah*. But when does this fight happen? When it is inevitable and unavoidable as the very integrity of a state, the lives of its citizens or the very ideology is facing a big danger. But a very baseless smear campaign is going on against *Jihad* and it is branded as a synonym to terrorism, so this book is a must to make the true concept of *Jihad* clear and counter the propaganda.

SHARIA AND POLITICS (ENGLISH)

Islam is *Deen* and *Deen* means a complete system and a perfect code of life as this is given by the very creator of the worlds, who knows all about his creatures, their qualities and their shortcomings, and can provide a perfect solution to their problems. But unfortunately, some people have been doing wrong in the name of *Khalafat* and presenting their wrong idea as the *Islamic* political system, so there was great need of a book that can present the proper shape of an *Islamic* state and *Islamic* political system given by the Creator; when executed properly, it is actually a mercy and blessing for the creatures. This book explains this concept clearly.

HAJJ & UMRAH IN ALL FOUR SCHOOLS OF JURISPRUDENCE (ENGLISH)

Hajj (pilgrimage to *Mecca*) is one of the Five Pillars of *Islam* and a very important but a complicated type of *Ibadah* (worship) as *Muslims* from all around the world get together to perform it together. They follow the interpretation of their *Imams* (jurists), so sometimes they look at others when they do not perform a specific virtue the way they do, then they think they are doing wrong, which is not so, but all of them are performing correctly according to the interpretation of their *Imams*. This book gives all these details in sequence according to all four *Imams* the *Muslim Ummah* follows.

MOON SIGHTING, SALATUL TARAWEEH AND SALATUL WITR (ENGLISH)

The *Islamic* Calendar is lunar-based. Its different *Ibadaat* time is based on moon-sighting; the lunar month starts with the new moon. Even though astronomy tells us what day the moon will be born (i.e., new) with perfect accuracy, discerning on which day it will be visible in a specific area is still not accurate. That is why differences in opinion happen all over the world, and should we to go by the calendar or by a sighting?

Also, at *Ramadan*, which is the most important month in *Islam* as a mandatory *Ibadah*, fasting is mandatory as well, but there is an extra, highly recommended *Ibadah,* the *Taraweeh*, but how many *Rakat* should we pray? *Muslims* differ about this. Another important *Ibadah* is *Salat Ul Witr*. We use this prayer all year, but during *Ramadan* this is prayed in *Jama'at* and different *Imams* have different opinions regarding the number of *Rakats* and its procedure. So, this book gives all the details about these three important issues.

SCIENCE OF HADITH (ENGLISH)

Hadith is the second fundamental source of *Islamic* law. They are the words, actions and sanctions of the *Holy Prophet*. To record all these in memory and writing, to compile it and to record the biography of those narrators who did this great job and this is considered as a miracle of the *Prophet*. But the enemies of *Islam* used to create doubts in this regard. This book is written on this subject, and it is enough an answer to all the objections that people made from different angles.

ABOUT THE AUTHOR

Qazi Fazl Ullah is an American philosopher, linguist, and author. He is *Fazil Wafaqul Madaris* where he studied *Arabic* grammar, *Arabic* literature, *Fiqh*, jurisprudence, logic, philosophy, *Ilmul Kalam, Seerah, Tafseer, Hadith,* and *Islamic* history. He studied at *Peshawar University* and *Islamic University Islamabad* in *Pakistan* and specialized in law, economics, and political science. He has taught all these subjects in *Pakistan* and the United States at different institutions. He was elected as a *National Assembly Parliamentarian* in *Pakistan*. He worked in underserved areas to provide jobs, build infrastructure, schools, museums, public health facilities, and increase communication technologies as the chair of the *Social Action Board*. He has traveled extensively throughout the Middle East, North Africa, Europe, South East Asia, North and Central America. He has given seminars in various parts of the world in these subjects. He speaks and has given lectures and seminars in *Urdu, Pashto, Farsi,* English, and *Arabic*. He has published works in *Pashto, Urdu, Arabic,* and English internationally. He has given the complete *Tafsir Ul Quran* in *Pashto* multiple times in *Pakistan*. He has also given *Tafsir Ul Quran* in *Urdu, Pashto,* and English in the United States. It includes *Usul Ul Fiqh, Usul Ul Mirath, Hadith al Qudsi, Hadith an Nabawi* in English on multiple occasions. He considers himself a student to continue acquisitions of knowledge. He is currently leading *Tafsir Ul Quran, Usual Al Fiqh, Seerat Un Nabi,* Science of Inheritance (*Mirath*) in English and *Al*

Mukhtar Lil Fatawa, Dirayat Ul Riwaya in *Arabic* in Los Angeles, California.

www.ingramcontent.com/pod-product-compliance
Lightning Source LLC
Chambersburg PA
CBHW022009160426
43197CB00007B/355